THE WORKBOOK OF
LIVING PRAYER

The Workbook of
Living Prayer

Maxie Dunnam

UPPER
ROOM BOOKS®
NASHVILLE

To
Jean Clegg Dickinson
and
Marguerite Glenn McKeithen

"A lifetime's not too long
to live as friends."

CONTENTS

Introduction   9
    An Adventure of Prayer   11
    Suggestions for First Group Meeting   13

Week One: Getting Our Bearings and Beginning the Adventure   15
    Daily Guides   19
    Group Meeting for Week One   35

Week Two: With Christ in the School of Prayer   39
    Daily Guides   42
    Group Meeting for Week Two   60

Week Three: When All Else Fails, Follow Directions   63
    Daily Guides   66
    Group Meeting for Week Three   86

Week Four: Basic Ingredients of Prayer and Discovering Your Pattern 89
    Daily Guides   93
    Group Meeting for Week Four   117

Week Five: Pray without Ceasing   119
    Daily Guides   122
    Group Meeting for Week Five   141

Week Six: Resources for Praying   145
    Daily Guides   150
    Group Meeting for Week Six   172

Appendix   175
    Three Additional Weeks of Study   175
    Scripture Cards   179

Notes   181

Bibliography   182

INTRODUCTION

T. S. Eliot, the world-renowned poet, was fond of telling how he hailed a London taxi one day and after being driven a short distance, the driver asked him: "Ain't you T. S. Eliot?" Replying in the affirmative, Eliot asked the driver how he recognized him. "Oh, I know a lot of famous people by sight," the cabbie said. "Why just the other day I picked up Lord Bertrand Russell. And I says to him, 'Lord Russell, what's it all about?' And you know he couldn't tell me."

I feel a bit that way in writing this introduction to the revision of *The Workbook of Living Prayer*. According to the publisher almost half a million of the workbooks have been printed. I'm humbled by that. I'm quite certain that when my days are over, my greatest contribution to the cause of Christianity and the Christian church will be *The Workbook of Living Prayer*. Through the years I've received literally thousands of letters from people who have used it and have expressed their appreciation; many of them have testified that their lives were transformed, and many others mark their commitment to full-time Christian ministry to the use of the workbook.

I've learned a lot during these past decades—but nothing more important than the fact that I am still *learning to pray*. That means that our life of prayer is a pilgrimage. I've never known anyone who was satisfied with his or her prayer life. What we might call "giants" in prayer—and I've been privileged to know a number of them—would never testify to anything but their ongoing desire to be closer to the Lord, to be more effective in their praying, to be more transparent in the presence of the One who "knows us inside and out."

The past decades have been turbulent ones. Things we would have never dreamed of have happened. One of the most dramatic and significant was the destruction of the Berlin Wall and the crumbling of an atheistic political and economic system that held a huge part of the world in its grip.

Over a seventy-year period, from the Russian Revolution of 1917, oppression and persecution played havoc with the church. The vast majority of church buildings in the Soviet Union were destroyed or closed. Christians were imprisoned and put to death, and some of them went "underground." I was in the Soviet Union in 1981 and came away frustrated and confused. I experienced pain to see beautiful churches turned into warehouses. I was depressed to see primarily elderly women in the few churches that were still open. Yet I was also thrilled at the Christian witness of the faithful and was challenged in my own faith by the story of their faithfulness. Through the years, one of the primary pictures I've had of the church was the picture of old women, grandmothers—they call them *babushka*—in their head scarves, sitting in the dark corners of the churches, sometimes dusting and polishing the altar and furniture of churches that were no longer dynamic places of worship. I kept asking myself, What can those grandmothers do? How can they keep alive the faith and the church? Where are the young people and how are the young people going to receive the Christian witness?

In 1986, two years before the celebration of the one thousandth anniversary of Christianity in Russia, a delegation of twenty-five priests and pastors did a sort of "trial run," visiting Russia two weeks before that huge event was to take place. The priests and pastors spent three hours going through customs as they argued their right to bring Russian-language Bibles into that country: some were confiscated, some were not. Dana Robert, in an article in *The Christian Century* (December 24, 1986), told about the visit of those twenty-five persons and how the majority of the believers they met in the churches were elderly women:

> Like the widows of old, these women are the backbone of the church, keeping it alive through their sacrificial offerings, prayers and physical services such as cleaning the buildings and planting flowers. When somebody asked a Russian priest whether it was healthy for the church to be composed of so many aged women, he replied with a story: "In the early days of communism," he said, "many churches were blown up and the priests, monks, and nuns were executed. Lenin argued that once the grandmothers died, nobody would remember that there had been a church in Russia. But now Lenin is long dead, and the church is still full of grandmothers who were children when he was alive. As long as the Russian church has its grandmothers, it will survive."

Since the fall of the Berlin Wall, the crumbling of the atheistic system of government and economics, on our visits to former Soviet Union countries we have heard a similar word. It has been the grandmothers—the *praying* grandmothers—who have kept the faith alive in all those countries. There is a thrilling story of the church in Plzen (in what was formerly Czechoslovakia). Through the years of Communist oppression and persecution of Christians, the membership of the largest Protestant church in that city dwindled to almost nothing. The building was taken over by the government and used by the university. There were a few faithful folks who continued to gather, primarily for prayer. About three years before the destruction of the wall, providentially four or five younger persons in their mid-twenties joined these seven or nine faithful few. These younger folks had been miraculously converted through an underground expression of the Christian church. This small group of approximately fourteen persons met weekly for prayer and became the nucleus of a revival in that city. When I was in Plzen in 1992, I preached and worshiped with one of the most dynamic Christian congregations I've ever known—and they testify that the source of that revival was those praying people.

The government has now given them back the building which they confiscated, and it is being renewed. It is a Methodist congregation called the Maranatha Church—a vibrant, dynamic witness to the faithfulness of Christians, especially the meaning and power of prayer. It is a convincing witness as to what this workbook is all about.

I learned recently that in what is now Bratislova, Slovakia (then Czechoslovakia), a Methodist preacher had translated this workbook and it has been used by him as a teaching resource among faithful Christians living under very limiting oppression. In 1983 it was translated in Taiwan into Chinese for the purpose of nurturing people in prayer and taking it into mainland China.

My prayer is that all who use this revised edition will learn not only something about prayer, but more than anything else will be inspired to pray. I am convinced that this is one of the most glorious privileges that is given to Christians—to enter the kingdom and to participate in the work of the kingdom through praying.

An Adventure of Prayer

Here is the plan. This is a six-week adventure. It is an individual journey, but my hope is that you will share it with some fellow-pilgrims who will meet together once each week during the six weeks of the study. You are asked to give twenty to thirty minutes each day to *work* at making prayer a living experience. For most persons this twenty to thirty minutes will come at the beginning of the day. However, if it is not possible for you to give the time at the beginning of your day, do it whenever the time is available.

I arranged the workbook in six major divisions, each to guide you for one week. These six major divisions contain seven sections, one for each day of the week.

In each day's section you will read something *about* prayer. Not too much, but I hope that it will be enough to provide something of the nature, meaning, and possibilities of prayer. Included in this will be some portions of scripture. It is my conviction that the scripture is a basic resource for Christian living and praying.

Then each day there will be a time for *reflecting and recording*. This dimension calls you to record some of your reflections. The degree of meaning you receive from this workbook is largely dependent upon your faithfulness to this practice. You may be unable on a particular day to do precisely what is requested. If so, then simply record that fact and make a note why you cannot follow through. This may give you insight about yourself that will mean growth.

Whatever the case may be, do not feel guilty. The emphasis is upon growth, not performance. So follow the content and directions seriously but not slavishly. Always remember that this is a personal pilgrimage. What you write is your private property. You do not have to share it with anyone. The importance of it is not what it may mean to someone else, but what it means to you. Writing, even if it is only brief notes or single-word reminders, helps us clarify our feelings and thinking. Such clarity is essential for prayer. (This means that every person must have a workbook. No two persons can share the same text.)

The significance of the *Reflecting and Recording* dimensions will grow as you move along. Even beyond the six-week period, you will find meaning in looking back to what you wrote on a particular day in response to a particular situation.

The third major aspect of the daily presentations is the *During the Day* instructions. Here you receive suggestions for making your prayer experience a part of your whole life. The dynamic of prayer is communion with God. The goal of prayer is a life of friendship and fellowship with God, cooperating with the Spirit, living God's will in the world. *During the Day* asks you to be intentional about moving from your specific time of prayer into a life of prayer by consciously seeking to relate all of life to God.

In the history of Christian piety the spiritual director or guide has been a significant person. To varying degrees, most of us have had spiritual directors—persons to whom we have turned for support and direction in our spiritual pilgrimage. There is a sense in which this workbook can be a spiritual guide. You can use it as a private venture without participating in a group.

Its meaning will be enhanced, however, if you share the adventure with eight to twelve others. In this way, the "priesthood of all believers" will come alive, and you will profit from the growing insights of others, and they from yours. A guide for group sharing is included in the text at the end of each week.

If this is a group venture, all persons should begin their personal involvement with the text on the same day. Therefore, when you come together as a group, all will have been dealing with the same material and will be at the same place in the text. It will be helpful if you have a get-acquainted group meeting to begin the adventure. A guide for this first meeting is given on page 13.

To prepare a workbook such as this, I have felt it necessary to make some basic assumptions. Primarily, I have *assumed* that God is, that God is good, and that communication with God is possible. These assumptions can be argued, but that is not the purpose of the workbook. We know that God is greater than our finite understanding, yet we cannot fully describe reality without a God who has essential personal characteristics such as love, purpose, power, and freedom. If these assumptions are problematical with you, I hope you will take your present understanding of God and your concepts of reality and try to fit them into these assumptions as an *experiment* for six weeks. In your reflection, wrestle with the ideas that are being presented, and try to experience the dynamic of communion with God, which is what prayer is all about. This will mean focused thinking and meditation. Involve yourself to the degree and in whatever fashion you can, always seeking to expand your understanding and experience by experimentation. To some, prayer itself is a theological problem. Again, the purpose of the workbook is experimental, not argumentative. My hope is that if you have problems with prayer itself, you will act as if prayer is a possibility and see where you come out!

Again let me emphasize that this is your unique pilgrimage. I hope you will become aware of your story. The workbook will achieve its purpose if it helps you in your journey of a living relationship with God. While we may share that journey with others, it must be uniquely personal. There is a classic story about a holy man in India who was bothered by mice playing around him where he meditated. To alleviate this irritation, he got a cat and tied it to a stake near him so that the mice would be scared away. He never explained to his disciples why the cat was staked out in his meditation room. So when they meditated, they thought they had to have a cat staked out near them. My hope is that you will not make their mistake in your use of this workbook.

There is nothing dogmatic, holy, or magical about anything that is suggested as an exercise or practice in this workbook. It is a means, not an end in itself. Take what is here, try it, live with it, and experiment with it in finding your way of living prayer.

I would like to acknowledge and thank The Upper Room staff and those who made a special contribution to the preparation of the original workbook. Those persons include: Dr. Wilson O. Weldon, Dr. Rueben Job, Reverend Danny Morris, Mrs. Lois Seifert, Reverend Stanley Smith, Reverend James Stewart, Mrs. Lenore Jerome, Dr. Barry Woodbridge, and Dr. Owen Owens.

Suggestions for First Group Meeting

Group sessions for this workbook are designed to last one and one-half hours (with the exception of this initial meeting). Those sharing in the group should covenant to attend all sessions unless an emergency prevents them. There will be seven weekly sessions with the first being a get-acquainted time.

A group consisting of eight to twelve members is about the right size. Larger numbers make it difficult for individual involvement.

One person can provide the leadership for the entire six weeks, or leaders can be assigned from week to week. The leader's task is to:

- model a style of openness, honesty, and warmth. (A leader should not ask others to share what he or she is not willing to share. Usually the leader should be the first to share, especially as it relates to personal experience.)
- moderate the discussion.
- encourage reluctant members to participate and try to prevent a few persons from doing all the talking.
- keep the sharing centered in personal experience, rather than academic debate.
- honor the time schedule. (If it appears necessary to go longer than one and one-half hours, the leader should get consensus for continuing another twenty or thirty minutes.)
- see that the meeting time and place are known by all, especially if meetings are held in different homes.

- make sure necessary materials for meetings are available and that a meeting room is arranged ahead of time.

It is desirable that weekly meetings be held in the homes of the participants. (Hosts will make sure that there are as few interruptions as possible, such as children, telephone, pets, etc.) If meetings are held in a church, it should be in an informal, comfortable setting. Participants are urged to dress casually, to be comfortable and relaxed.

If refreshments are served, this should come after the meeting. In this way, those who wish to stay longer for informal discussion may do so, while those who need to adhere to the time schedule will be free to leave but will get full value of the formal meeting time.

Since the initial meeting is for the purpose of getting acquainted and beginning the prayer pilgrimage, here is a way to get started.

1. Have each person in the group give his or her full name and the name by which each wishes to be called. Do away with titles. Address all persons by their first name or nickname. (You should make a list of the names somewhere in your workbook.)

2. Let each person in the group tell about one of the happiest, most exciting, or most meaningful experiences he or she has had during the past three or four weeks. After each person has shared in this way, let the entire group sing the *Doxology* ("Praise God, from Whom All Blessings Flow") or "Hallelu, Hallelu, Hallelu, Hallelujah, Praise Ye the Lord."

3. After this experience of happy sharing, ask each person who is willing to tell his or her expectations of the pilgrimage. Why did he or she become a part of it? What does each expect to gain from it? What are the reservations?

4. The leader should now review the introduction to the workbook and ask if there are questions about directions and procedures. (This means that the leader should have read the introduction prior to the meeting.) If persons have not received copies of the workbook, the books should be handed out now. *Remember that every person must have his or her own workbook.*

5. Day One in the workbook is the day following this initial meeting, and the next meeting should be held on Day Seven of the first week. If the group must choose another weekly meeting time other than seven days from this initial session, the reading assignment should be brought into harmony with that so that the weekly meetings are always on Day Seven, and Day One is always the day following a weekly meeting.

6. After checking to see that everyone knows the time and place of the next meeting, the leader may close with a prayer, thanking God for each person in the group, for the opportunity for growth, and for the possibility of learning to pray.

Week One

Getting Our Bearings and Beginning the Adventure

INTRODUCTION
WEEK ONE

Accept the Mystery and the Power!

My oldest grandchild, Nathan, celebrated his eighth birthday on September 25, 1994. When he came to visit us with his parents and his sisters during the summer of 1993, we played baseball in the backyard. Now that's a normal kind of thing to do—a grandfather pitching a ball to his grandson, then chasing the ball and pitching it again. But every time I play baseball with Nathan, I almost cry with joy that he can hit that ball with great precision and regularity.

There was a time when we were told that would never be the case. When Nathan was three months old, his parents noticed that his eyes were moving around a lot, never quite focusing on anything. They took him to a pediatric ophthalmologist, who told them that Nathan had a congenital problem called nystagmus and that his eyes would always basically be that way. He then dilated Nathan's eyes and looked inside. In a matter-of-fact manner the ophthalmologist told Nathan's mother, Kim, that Nathan had another congenital problem called optic nerve hypoplasia. This is a very rare defect in which Nathan's optic nerves were only about half the size they needed to be in order for him to see normally.

"What does that mean?" Kim asked. "Oh well, of course," the doctor went on as if he were discussing the weather, "he'll never be able to see normally; it's an uncorrectable problem. He will probably have to go to a special school and things like that. But don't be too worried; sometimes it's only minor, and they can go to regular school and sit in front of the class and things like that."

. . . and things like that?—Kim thought—*Doctor, are you crazy? This is my son you are talking about.*

You can imagine the anguish of those who knew and loved Nathan, the pain and frustration that followed.

When I got that word, naturally I began to pray, and I invited people to pray. The word went out on The Upper Room Prayer Ministry network, as well as the other networks of our family. And people all over the nation began to pray for Nathan.

After numerous tests, it was confirmed that Nathan had the problem. At that point there was nothing to do but to live with it and to prepare for a little boy moving through life with very limited eyesight.

About a year later, Kim and John, with Nathan, had moved to another city, Hartford, Connecticut. They followed up with a doctor for Nathan there. They gave him the medical records, and he examined Nathan and was pleased with the outcome. Kim was reassured, but not overly excited. Then the doctor dilated Nathan's eyes. "Great!" he said. "These optic nerves look nice and pink and healthy."

In a sermon Kim preached much later, she talked about this experience:

> *What?* I thought. *Say that again!* I almost dropped Nathan in astonishment. I suggested that maybe he should read the first doctor's report more closely; after all, he had used words like "thin" and "white" to describe the optic nerves. Well, the doctor was amazed, because what he saw and what the first doctor reported were on opposite poles. And not only that, but the nystagmus that supposedly would never disappear had diminished remarkably. And now, while it is still there, it is not always very noticeable.
>
> Of course, in the world of medicine, there must be confirmation as well as explanation. So we went to a third doctor to get his opinion, and he too agreed that there was no optic nerve hypoplasia. They were both baffled about the drastic difference. But somehow, after the initial surprise wore off, I didn't feel very baffled. On the surface it appeared that the original doctor had made a mistake. Nathan hadn't been exactly helpful during the exam; in fact, he had been quite angry that we had the audacity to try to hold him down. So maybe the doctor didn't see clearly. But that's a drastic diagnosis to make if you didn't see very clearly. And he was an awfully good doctor, highly regarded in medical circles; the doctors (in Hartford) even know him. Could this be more than a mistake? Could this be the grace of God?
>
> When Nathan was first diagnosed, we told our friends and family, who in turn told their friends and families. Soon we were receiving letters from all over the world saying that Nathan was being included in the daily prayers of many, many people. Could this also be an example of the power of prayer?
>
> I realize that I'm treading on difficult ground here as I touch on the topic of the power of prayer. However, I'm reminded of today's lesson from the Hebrew Scriptures: "For my thoughts are not your thoughts, neither are your ways my ways, says the LORD." There is a divine mystery here that we cannot fathom in human terms. We cannot reduce God to a human scale; nor can we assume that because events such as this do not happen all the time, they don't happen at all.

But I told this story for a reason. I believe that Nathan received God's grace. I believe my husband, John, and I received God's grace. And it had *nothing* to do with merit. For I know that if merit were the deciding factor, I would not be standing today; nor would Nathan's eyes have been healed. My life is as stained and tarnished as anyone else's. And what great work could Nathan have done at his young age that could possibly have deserved God's grace? That is the beauty and the paradox of grace: God does not demand that we *earn* God's blessings. The grace and love of God transcend our human ability to understand. But even without understanding, we are called to accept that gift of grace, freely given, and rejoice.

I'm sure you can understand why I can hardly keep from crying when I play with Nathan; and when he hits the ball three out of four times, I know he sees very well.

Now there is a mystery here, and that word needs to be spoken. Not all folks for whom we pray are healed. I don't understand that. I've prayed for people who did experience healing. In fact, every Sunday evening at our church, we have a time of prayer when we lay hands on people and anoint them with oil and pray for their healing—the healing of their bodies, their minds, their emotions, their relationships. Healing doesn't always come—especially in the way for which we pray. Some of the people for whom we pray die. There is a great mystery. But what we also need to know and believe is that there is great power. Things happen when we pray that do not happen if we don't pray.

My experience with Nathan is a dramatic one, and I don't share it very often because it is so dramatic. And when I share it, I'm always quick to say that the outcome of our praying is not always the same. I underscore the mystery. However, I share it to make the case that there is mystery and power in prayer. Prayer is one of the ways we link ourselves with God, we put ourselves in the channel of God's moving power, and we participate with God in ministry to all persons.

DAY ONE

It Is Natural to Pray

You may or may not have had a meal today. But before the day is past you will have eaten something—probably three meals, and maybe a snack between. Eating is natural and necessary.

If you haven't eaten today, chances are you have had a cup of coffee or tea, or a glass of water or milk. Drinking is natural and necessary.

Like eating and drinking, prayer is not something foreign to our human nature. Prayer is perhaps the deepest impulse of the human soul.

Samuel Johnson was once asked what was the strongest argument for prayer. He replied, "There is no argument for prayer." He did not mean that prayer is irrational or that there are not convincing arguments for the practice of it, but that prayer is natural and universal. We all pray, and we pray because it is a part of our native endowment.

Prayer is related to our search for meaning, our longing for relationship, our need to grow. Prayer, however practiced, is an expression of our hunger for God. This hunger is a part of who we are. Augustine's word is more than a pious cliché: "For thee were we made, O God, and our hearts are restless until they find their rest in thee."

Again and again the psalmist reminds us of the naturalness and universality of our hunger for God.

Psalm 63:1

O God, you are my God, I seek you,
my soul thirsts for you;
my flesh faints for you,
as in a dry and weary land
where there is no water.

In the Sermon on the Mount, Jesus recognizes this natural hungering after God. More than that, he claims this hungering will be satisfied.

Matthew 5:6

Blessed are those who hunger and thirst for righteousness,
for they will be filled.

Reflecting and Recording

A part of our adventure is reflecting and recording. The importance of written notes will grow in meaning as we move along. Reflect and record in response to this guidance.

1. Our society offers us an abundance of food and drink on a twenty-four-hour basis. Have you ever been deprived of this abundance and really experienced hunger or thirst? What did it feel like when you finally found nourishment?

2. All of us hunger for God. How does that hunger express itself in your life? List two or three ways.

3. How do you see the hunger affecting others? Think of specific persons. Name them, and in a phrase or sentence indicate how that hunger is manifesting itself in them.

4. Looking at others often helps us look at ourselves. Write two or three sentences describing how you feel right now about your hunger for God.

5. As you begin this adventure, consider this word from the letter of James: "If any of you is lacking in wisdom, ask God, who gives to all generously and ungrudgingly, and it will be given you" (James 1:5).

I believe that the Holy Spirit of God is the great teacher. I have trusted the Spirit in preparing this workbook. Your part is to trust God to use this process to help you learn to pray. Right now, in your own heart, make this affirmation:

I want to learn to pray.
I open my mind to you, God.
Teach me to pray.

During the Day

If your mind comes back to this experience any time during this day or night, try to remember the persons you named in whom you have seen the hunger for God working. Simply ask God to bless them and satisfy their longing. Be open to God's using you in meeting their need.

DAY TWO

It Is Not Easy to Pray

As *living* beings, we breathe, we eat, we drink, we sleep. As *human* beings we breathe, eat, drink, sleep, *and pray*. It's part of our nature as human beings to pray. This is one of the ways we express our natural hungering for God. Natural it is; easy it isn't!

There is a difference between the tendency to pray and the practice of prayer. We have the tendency to pray—the reflexive crying out in the face of pain or trouble; the spontaneous shout of joy in the presence of beauty, accomplishment, fulfillment. We give expression to it sporadically according to the moods and circumstances of our life.

To live a life of prayer is something else. To pray consistently is not easy. It requires commitment and discipline. Don't condemn yourself if you find praying difficult. Most of us do. Even those whom we call *saints* found or find praying difficult. Read their journals and confessions, and you will find them struggling, searching, wrestling, seeking to make the natural tendency to pray become a natural practice in everyday life. Jesus' disciples didn't find it easy.

Mark 14:32-42

They went to a place called Gethsemane; and [Jesus] said to his disciples, "Sit here while I pray." He took with him Peter and James and John, and began to be distressed and agitated. And he said to them, "I am deeply grieved, even to death; remain here, and keep awake." And going a little farther, he threw himself on the ground and prayed that, if it were possible, the hour might pass from him. He said, "Abba, Father, for you all things are possible; remove this cup from me; yet, not what I want, but what you want." He came and found them sleeping; and he said to Peter, "Simon, are you asleep? Could you not keep awake one hour? Keep awake and pray that you may not come into the time of trial; the spirit indeed is willing, but the flesh is weak." And again he went away and prayed, saying the same words. And once more he came and found them sleeping, for their eyes were very heavy; and they did not know what to say to him. He came a third time and said to them, "Are you still sleeping and taking your rest? Enough! The hour has come; the Son of Man is betrayed into the hands of sinners. Get up, let us be going. See, my betrayer is at hand."

Discipline, then, is a part of the life of prayer. The purpose of discipline, however, is to enhance and increase the spontaneous dimension of praying.

Reflecting and Recording

1. Think about the last two years of your life. In the space above the time line below, write the letter (**H** = high, **M** = medium, or **L** = low) that best describes your prayer life in terms of highs and lows during that time period.

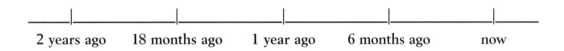

2 years ago   18 months ago   1 year ago   6 months ago   now

2. Identify and write here the major circumstances or events in the high and low periods of your prayer life.

3. What primary difficulties do you have in prayer?

During the Day

Think about this: Christ wants me to pray naturally, but he understands my difficulties in praying in a disciplined way. He wants me to find a creative discipline that frees me to pray more deeply and meaningfully.

Yesterday you named some people and noted how you see the hunger for God manifested in them. Did you remember them during the day? Why not call them on the phone, or write them a note today? If you feel comfortable doing so, you may tell them precisely why you are calling or writing (this will be a good way to share your own experience with them), or you may simply let them know that you are thinking of them and that you care about them. This kind of response will make your praying a *living* experience.

DAY THREE

"O Taste and See That the Lord Is Good"

Psalm 34:4-8

I sought the LORD, and he answered
        me,
        and delivered me from all my fears.
Look to him, and be radiant;
        so your faces shall never be
        ashamed.
This poor soul cried, and was heard
        by the LORD,
        and was saved from every
        trouble.
The angel of the LORD encamps
        around those who fear him, and
        delivers them.
O taste and see that the LORD is good.

As you continue your adventure today, spend five minutes in silence thinking about that one phrase: "O taste and see that the LORD is good." Don't argue in your mind about whether you would express this thought in the same way; just get at the thought itself. Let it tumble around and say to you what it has to say. As you begin your silence now, repeat the phrase five times as follows (emphasize word(s) underlined in each statement):

O <u>taste</u> and <u>see</u> that the LORD is good!
O taste and see that the <u>LORD</u> is good!
O taste and see that the LORD <u>is</u> good!
O taste and see that the LORD is <u>good</u>!
<u>O taste and see that the LORD is good</u>

In the margin, make notes on what comes to you in your silence. Every time you come to this sign (■ ■ ■) in the workbook, please stop for reflection, for prayer, and follow the suggestions before you move on in your reading.

In prayer, we begin with God and end with God. *The God to whom we pray is good!* This great and unique assertion of the Christian faith is a primary foundation upon which we build our life of prayer. We know that God's goodness in giving us life and our world has been misused for evil purposes. We often experience much that is not good. Yet God always offers us the good in all circumstances. This is exactly what Jesus said in some of his boldest words about prayer: "If you then, who are evil, know how to give good gifts to your children, how much more will your Father . . . give good things to those who ask him!" (Matt. 7:11). *The God to whom we pray is good.*

Reflecting and Recording

My understanding of the meaning of "God is good" has expanded through the years. The Bible affirms the goodness of God, but for much of my life I thought of that in terms of God's being "religiously good." The "goodness of God" was more *descriptive* than *practical.*

Our praying changes when we realize that God's "being good" is at least like our "being good." To be good is at least to live up to the highest and best we know. Add to that the fact that God must certainly know what is the highest good of all and that to be good is to do good. We can trust our lives to such a "good" God.

1. Look at prayer as you have practiced it. Has it been rooted in the conviction that God is good? What does this say about the way many of us *beg* God to do something?

2. Augustine said, "[God] loves every one as though there were but one of us to love." (Think of five simple phrases that register your response to this fact, such as "Never thought of it that way," "Hard to believe," etc.)

    a.

    b.

    c.

d.

e.

During the Day

"O taste and see that the LORD is good." Put this truth into your own words (such as "May all my senses experience that the Lord is good"), repeat it to yourself and think about it as often as you can bring it to mind.

DAY FOUR

God Is Good, and I Can Communicate with God

"O taste and see that the LORD is good." God is good and wants to give good gifts to us. This is a primary assumption in prayer.

A second assumption is that *communication with God is possible.* That seems so simple and so obvious, but is it? This has been one of the greatest difficulties in my life—to believe that I could actually talk with God and that God would *hear* and *listen* and *respond* to me.

This is an enormous assumption that needs to be fixed firmly in our minds at the outset of this adventure in prayer. What it means is that I, among all the millions of people in the world, can have personal communication with the Father.

The dominant image of God in the New Testament is *father.* This was Jesus' descriptive word about God's nature. In the Sermon on the Mount, he used this figure to help us get our concerns into perspective.

Matthew 6:25-26

Therefore, I tell you, do not worry about your life, what you will eat or what you will drink, or about your body, what you will wear. Is not life more than food, and the body more than clothing? Look at the birds of the air; they neither sow nor reap nor gather into barns, and yet your heavenly Father feeds them. Are you not of more value than they?

God is like a shepherd who misses even one lost sheep from the flock, like a homemaker who sweeps a house clean to find one lost coin, like a father who grieves for one prodigal son who has left home (Luke 15). "It is not the will of your Father in heaven that one of these little ones should be lost" (Matt. 18:14).

Take five minutes and think about that. God cares for each one of us as individuals. Is it hard for you to accept that? Do you believe it? Have you been praying as though you believe it? God cares for _____. (Write your full name in the blank.) Take three minutes now, and center your attention on this monumental truth.

■ ■ ■

One of the characteristics of a caring father is the desire to communicate with his children. This desire to communicate may be expressed directly (as in the interest and concern shown in being with them) or indirectly (as in times when the father withholds the wisdom of his experience so as to encourage his children to think and judge for themselves). If God is like a father, then communication, directly or indirectly, must be at the heart of our relationship.

Reflecting and Recording

Meditate now upon God as a caring father who wants to communicate with you. God wants to hear about what you are feeling, thinking, and desiring. If you really believe that, what are the five most important things you would like to say to God?

1.
2.
3.
4.
5.

In a closing prayer say "thank you" to God in whatever way you would say thank you to a caring father.

During the Day

God, like a caring father, wants to stay in touch with God's children. During the day, remember:

— God is good;
— God cares;
— God desires communication with you.

Find a few quiet minutes at different times during this day and simply talk to God about what's important to you today.

DAY FIVE

Prayer Is a Privilege, Not a Duty

What you have been experiencing the past four days, indeed your entire past experience in prayer, will determine your response to the great idea we want to consider today: *Prayer is a privilege, not a duty.*

Earlier this week we thought about how discipline seems to take the spontaneity out of prayer. Many of us see prayer as a discipline, as a duty, something we must do. We've been taught that we *ought* to pray, and when we don't, we feel guilty. We will take a giant step forward in our adventure when we cease seeing prayer as a duty and begin to look upon it as a privilege. As a privilege, the discipline of praying becomes a creative freedom, not a bondage of duty. Consider this testimony of Sir Wilfred Grenfell:

> The privilege of prayer to me is one of the most cherished possessions, because faith and experience alike convince me that God sees and answers, and [God's] answers I never venture to criticize. It is only my part to ask. It is entirely [God's] to give or withhold, as [God] knows best. If it were otherwise, I would not dare to pray at all. In the quiet of home, in the heat of life and strife, in the face of death, the privilege of speech with God is inestimable. I value it more because it calls for nothing that the wayfaring [one], though a fool, cannot give—that is, the simplest expression to [one's] simplest desire. When I can neither see, nor hear, nor speak, still I can pray so that God can hear. When I finally pass through the valley of the shadow of death, I expect to pass through it in conversation with [God].[1]

There is a lot in this; reread it slowly.

■ ■ ■

Put that testimony of a great Christian disciple alongside the word from the psalmist whose hunger for God we encountered on the first day of our prayer adventure:

Psalm 63:1-8

O God, you are my God, I seek you,
my soul thirsts for you;
my flesh faints for you,
as in a dry and weary land
where there is no water.

So I have looked upon you in the
    sanctuary,
        beholding your power and glory.
Because your steadfast love is better
    than life,
        my lips will praise you.
So I will bless you as long as I live;
    I will lift up my hands and call
        on your name.

My soul is satisfied as with a
    rich feast,
        and my mouth praises you with
            joyful lips
when I think of you on my bed,
    and meditate on you in
        the watches of the night;
        for you have been my help,
    and in the shadow of your wings
        I sing for joy.
My soul clings to you;
    your right hand upholds me.

Like love and friendship, music, books, art, laughter, and play, prayer is a privilege, a great opportunity to be sought. Not to pray is an act of self-robbery. We are free to pray. The privilege is open to all of us. The privilege is communion with God through Christ, being aware of God's guidance. Try to experience God's presence now.

Get in a relaxed position. You may want to lie on your back. If you choose to sit, put both feet on the floor. Adjust yourself in the chair so that you are comfortable. Close your eyes and imagine Christ present with you.

Repeat aloud, but quietly, three times: *Jesus Christ, Jesus Christ, Jesus Christ.* Now very quietly, deliberately, reverently, with long pauses between each sounding, repeat three times: *Jesus Christ, Jesus Christ, Jesus Christ.*

Continue to imagine Christ's presence with you, and be quiet in his presence for two or three minutes.

Now read Psalm 23 aloud, slowly and deliberately.

KJV:

The LORD is my shepherd; I shall not want.
He maketh me to lie down in green pastures: he leadeth me beside the still
    waters.
He restoreth my soul: he leadeth me in the paths of righteousness for his name's
    sake.

Yea, though I walk through the valley of the shadow of death, I will fear no
evil: for thou art with me; thy rod and thy staff they comfort me.
Thou preparest a table before me in the presence of mine enemies: thou anointest
my head with oil; my cup runneth over.
Surely goodness and mercy shall follow me all the days of my life: and I will
dwell in the house of the LORD *for ever.*

Stay quiet now, letting the thoughts fill your mind and heart. You may want
to go back and read it quietly again and pause to ponder the particular words that
have special meaning to you today. Lay your workbook down and spend five or ten
minutes thinking about this psalm.

■ ■ ■

Reflecting and Recording

Did you have trouble practicing that kind of "thought-centering" for five minutes?
That's OK. We are learning; God accepts us where we are.

1. Writing your response to the following question will help you reflect upon
what you have experienced in your consideration of Psalm 23. Have you actually
felt God present with you in these past few minutes?

At what point did you begin to sense God's presence?

2. A number of images are present in Psalm 23: a shepherd leading us, green
pastures, still waters, restoration of the soul, paths of righteousness, shadow of
death, comfort, anointing with oil, a running-over cup. Name the images that are
especially meaningful to you. What are their meanings?

Thank God for God's presence with you now and ask for a sensitivity to God's presence during the next twenty-four hours.

■ ■ ■

During the Day

Before you leave your place now, select three specific times during the next twenty-four hours when you will deliberately seek to be conscious of God's presence (as you go to coffee break, as you go to or from work, while you are waiting for an appointment, during a mealtime, etc.). Write them down as an act of commitment.

1.
2.
3.

DAY SIX

Pray to Experience God As Real

1. As you begin this time alone today, reflect upon your experience yesterday. Did you follow through with seeking to be conscious of God's presence during the day as suggested? What meaning did it have? Evaluate how you did with that exercise. Use this space for your evaluation and response.

2. Recall the other days of our adventure. You may want to review some of the things you've written on those days. Be honest with yourself, and write a few sentences about what you are feeling concerning this adventure, the creative discipline it calls for, the problems you have encountered. Then ask God to help you make creative use of these experiences as you continue this adventure.

The first sentence of Psalm 63 is a great personal claim: "O God, you are my God." The heart of prayer is communion. *Communion* means being with, in union, sharing. Go back and read the part of Psalm 63 printed in the workbook for yesterday.

Nothing is real in our experience except those things with which we habitually deal. Persons say that they do not pray because God is not real to them. A truer statement would be that God is not real because they do not pray. Harry Emerson Fosdick puts this graphically:

> The practice of prayer is necessary to make God not merely an idea held in the mind but a Presence recognized in the life. In an exclamation that came from the heart of personal religion, the psalmist cried, "O God, thou art *my* God" (Psalm 63:1). To stand afar off and say "O God" is neither difficult nor searching . . . but it is an inward and searching matter to say, "O God, thou art *my* God." The first is theology, the second is religion; the first involves only opinion, the second involves vital experience; the first can be reached by thought, the second must be reached by prayer; the first leaves God afar off, the second alone makes [God] real. To be sure, all Christian service where we consciously ally ourselves with God's purpose, and all insight into history where we see God's providence at work, help to make God real to us; but there is an inward certainty of God that can come only from personal communion with God.[2]

Is this a new thought to you? Have you failed to pray consistently because God did not seem real to you? What an insight: *God does not seem real because we do not pray.* Do you see the implication of that? If we want to realize God, we must pray. Ponder that for a few minutes. It is a valuable thought *about* God. How does it fit in to your experience *of* God?

■ ■ ■

It may be that we will never learn to pray, never have any ongoing, creatively disciplined prayer life until our desire for communion with God is so great that we will be driven to prayer. Consider that thought for a few minutes. How great is your hunger for communion with God?

■ ■ ■

Reflecting and Recording

We began this adventure with this affirmation:

I want to learn to pray.
I open my mind to you, God.
Teach me to pray.

Can you turn that into an ardent prayer?

O God, I want you to be *my* God. I want you to be real to me as a vital experience. I am beginning to realize that such an experience can be mine through prayer. So teach me to pray.

Write such a prayer in your own words.

During the Day

Take this prayer with you all through this day:
     "O God, you are my God."

DAY SEVEN

Prayer Is Relationship

Prayer is relationship. It is *being* with God. It is *meeting*. It is a personal relationship in which you and God move from a *hello* of politeness to an *embrace* of love. It is communion. All other dimensions of prayer must take second place to this primary dimension.

Relationship is a personal matter. In prayer we are relating specifically to God who claims our total allegiance, calling us to love with all our heart, soul, and might: "Hear, O Israel: The LORD is our God, the LORD alone. You shall love the LORD your God with all your heart, and with all your soul, and with all your might" (Deut. 6:4-5).

Archbishop Anthony Bloom talks about this in a provocative way. He says that a relationship becomes meaningful and real the moment you begin to single out a person from the crowd. Prayer becomes real when it is no longer a relationship in the third person but in the first and second persons, when God becomes more than the remote "The Almighty," and becomes the singular and unique "Thou" or "You." The psalmist had discovered this: "O God, you are *my* God."

Anthony Bloom carries this analogy of name to the ultimate in personal relationship: We name a person what he or she means to us. This may be a nickname. He says David reached this point when he cried out to God, "O you, my joy!"

Psalm 91:1-2

You who live in the shelter of the Most High,
   who abide in the shadow of the Almighty,
will say to the LORD, "My refuge and my fortress;
   my God, in whom I trust."

Psalm 27:1:

The LORD is my light and my salvation;
   whom shall I fear?
The LORD is the stronghold of my life;
   of whom shall I be afraid?

The point is that prayer is reaching its height when we name God out of our experience of God: "O you, my joy!" "O God, my rock!" "O wonderful Savior."

And this naming of God determines how we experience God! Some can only name God in ways that lead to their experiencing him as enemy or absentee landlord. But as we come to know God in Jesus and in our relationship with God, we can experience the ever-loving God as our most intimate friend.

This naming can transform and put depth into our praying. We can be honest to God. Prayer then becomes the sorting out of our feelings as we bring them to God who cares and understands. It is the clarifying of our wishes and our needs and getting perspective in light of God's love and will.

Let's be specific in our experience of this relationship today.

Reflecting and Recording

1. How will you address God today? By what name or names will you call God?

2. Not only does relationship mean *naming* God for what God is to us, but it means trusting the relationship and bringing our feelings to God who cares and understands. What feelings or needs do you bring to God today?

3. What about your wishes? Lay those out specifically before God. Jot them down.

Look at your wishes now in light of God's love and what you believe is God's will. Do you believe now that your wishes are in harmony with God's love and will? Then joyously ask God to grant your wishes.

During the Day

This may be your toughest assignment yet, but try it. Select a person with whom you have a close relationship, a person you trust, someone with whom you will be spending a little time today (or make the opportunity to spend some time with such a person). Talk to that person about your prayer-adventure. Especially identify and discuss the similarities of your relationship with your friend to your relationship with God. (If you have trouble with this, go back and reread today's instructions about prayer as relationship.)

If you are participating in a group, read the following directions so that you will be familiar with what may be expected of you.

Group Meeting for Week One

Introduction

These group sessions will be most meaningful as they reflect the experience of all the participants. The guide is simply an effort to facilitate personal sharing. Therefore, do not be rigid in following these suggestions. The leader, especially, should seek to be sensitive to what is going on in the lives of the participants and to focus the group sharing on those experiences. Ideas are important. We should wrestle with new ideas, as well as with ideas with which we disagree. It is important, however, that the group meeting not become a debate about ideas. The emphasis should be upon persons—experiences, feelings, and meaning.

As the group comes to the place where all can share honestly and openly about what is happening in their lives, the more meaningful the experience will be. This does not mean sharing only the good or positive; share also the struggles, the difficulties, the negatives. Building a life of prayer involves struggle and change. We may not always *feel* God's presence. Therefore, praying is not dependent upon feeling. Don't be afraid to tell about your dry periods, your valleys, your plateaus, as well as your mountains.

Sharing Together

1. You may begin your time together by allowing time for each person in the group to talk about his or her most meaningful day with the workbook this week. The leader should begin this sharing. Tell why that particular day was so meaningful.

2. Now share your most difficult day. Tell what you experienced, and why it was so difficult.

3. Much of what we know and have experienced of prayer has come through other persons. Which person, in your experience, has had the most influence on your prayer life? Tell not only the name but how he or she influenced you. Was it because prayers were answered? Was it simple faith? a loving spirit? absolute trust? perseverance? discipline? joy?

4. Some of us have difficulties and hang-ups with prayer because of past experiences. Is there a "skeleton" in your prayer closet—someone or some experience that affected your prayer life negatively? Name the skeleton, and tell how you overcame or are presently wrestling with the negative experience.

5. Let each person in the group tell the most meaningful prayer experience of his or her life.

Praying Together

Corporate prayer is one of the great blessings of Christian community. Next week we will deal with Jesus' saying, "If two of you shall agree . . . ." There is power in corporate prayer, and it is important that this dimension be included in our prayer pilgrimage.

It is also important that you feel comfortable in this and that no pressure be placed on anyone to pray aloud. Silent corporate prayer is as vital and meaningful as verbal corporate prayer. Plan to spend at least fifteen minutes (usually at the close) of each group meeting in corporate prayer.

God does not need to hear our verbal words to hear our prayers. Silence, where thinking is centered and attention is focused, may provide our deepest periods of prayer. There is power, however, in a community on a common journey verbalizing their thoughts and feelings to God in the presence of their fellow pilgrims.

Verbal prayers should be offered spontaneously as a person chooses to pray aloud—not "let's go around the circle now, and each one pray."

Suggestions for this praying together time will be given each week. The leader for the week should regard these only as suggestions. What is happening in the meeting—the mood, the needs that are expressed, the timing—should determine the direction of the group praying together. Here are some possibilities for this closing period.

1. Let the group think back over the sharing that has taken place during this session. What personal needs or concerns came out of the sharing? Begin to speak these aloud—any person verbalizing a need or a concern that has been expressed. Don't hesitate to mention a concern that you may have picked up from another, "Mary isn't able to be with us this week because her son is in the hospital. Let's pray for her son and for her."

It will be helpful for each person to make notes of the concerns and needs that are mentioned. Enter deliberately into a period of silence. Let the leader verbalize each of these needs successively, allowing for a brief period following each so that persons in the group may center their attention and focus their prayer on the person, need, or concern mentioned. All of this will be in silence as each person prays in his or her own way.

2. Let the leader close this time of sharing by saying something like this: "One day this week we dealt with the thought that 'God loves every one as though there were but one of us to love.' Let's close this period of praying together by having as many of you as will simply give a word or a phrase that registers your response to that statement as it relates to God loves *you* as though *you* were the only one to love. Give your response aloud, and let us pause briefly between each response." When as many as wish have shared, the leader may say something like, "Let us affirm the love of God by saying together, 'Amen.'"

Week Two

With Christ in the School of Prayer

INTRODUCTION
WEEK TWO

The Way Jesus Prayed

During this week, our focus is on the instruction Jesus gave us about prayer. All of this is very important, and I'm sure you will find great meaning in it. But there are some things that need to be said. More than telling us about prayer, Jesus modeled prayer. It was not what Jesus said that caused the disciples to ask him to teach them to pray; it was the way they saw him praying.

Oftentimes Jesus went off by himself to pray. The disciples noticed that. In a very regular fashion, Jesus was alone with God. I am inspired by that. In my own life, I find that it is absolutely essential to be alone with God.

His most dramatic demonstration of prayer that teaches us so much about the nature of prayer is in the garden of Gethsemane. You know the story. Jesus had finished his celebration of Passover with the disciples. It was the night that he would be betrayed. The cross was looming ominously over his life path. So Jesus did as he always did; he prayed. He took several of his disciples with him but left them in one place and went further into the garden to be alone. And there, according to scripture, Jesus' anguish was so intense, his struggle so weighty, that his sweat became like drops of blood as he prayed. And you know the climax of that praying: "Not my will, but thine, be done" (Luke 22:42, KJV). It wasn't that Jesus wanted to go to the cross—certainly not: in fact, he prayed that "this cup pass from me." But the climax of his praying was submission. "Not my will, but thine, be done."

Here is what I am learning: Though the will of God may be tough and demanding, it is not to be *dreaded*. It bothers me that even the way we talk about God's will is a turn-off to those who have not yet trusted the Lord in making a Christian commitment. If we Christians who profess to know and trust God *dread* God's will, is it any wonder that those we want to become Christians, those who are yet "outside" the faith, look on the will of God as something to be feared and resisted?

As I write this, I am going through the most painful transition in ministry I have known. I have been the pastor of Christ Church in Memphis for twelve years, and I am leaving to become president of Asbury Theological Seminary. To make this move has been a wrenching decision. I am certain of God's call, but that does not relieve my pain and sadness. I don't yet understand why God has called, but I am excited about the unveiling of God's will in this new arena of service. Providentially, I believe, I was preaching a series of sermons on prayer as I wrestled with this call. One of those sermons had to do with prayer and God's will and guidance. My affirmation to the congregation has served me well during this chaotic time in my life: *God's will will not take us where God's grace will not sustain us.*

This week and in the weeks ahead, examine your whole life, specifically your prayer life, against how you feel and think about God's will. Does your brow furrow? Do you grit your teeth and steel yourself for the worst when you pray "Thy will be done"?

DAY ONE

"When You Pray, Go into a Room by Yourself"

Matthew 6:5-6, NEB

When you pray, do not be like the hypocrites; they love to say their prayers standing up in synagogue and at the street-corners, for everyone to see them. I tell you this: they have their reward already. But when you pray, go into a room by yourself, shut the door, and pray to your Father who is there in the secret place; and your Father who sees what is secret will reward you.

We began this adventure by saying that ultimately the Holy Spirit is the great teacher. God is the beginning and end of prayer. Since Jesus is the revelation of God, we can look to him as the revealer of a life of prayer and also as the teacher who has God's unique instruction for us.

Because prayer was such an important part of Jesus' life, it is no wonder that he had some strong directives about it in the Sermon on the Mount. He spoke about prayer on many occasions, but Matthew indicates the essentials of his teachings were set forth at the beginning of his public ministry.

When you pray, go into a room by yourself, shut the door, and pray to your Father who is there in the secret place.

It is clear from this word of Jesus that prayer is a personal matter. It is the communication that goes on between God and me. The emphasis here is upon *solitude*.

Now there is a difference between being alone and being alone *with God*. Even in the hectic, crowded conditions in which many of us live, most of us are often alone. Jesus is urging us to choose aloneness, to find solitude for a purpose: to be alone *with God*.

If we are going to have a life of prayer, Jesus is insistent that we must go into our room, shut the door, and be alone with God. To be alone with God is creative, purposeful solitude. This doesn't mean that we have to be behind a physical door to meet this condition. The emphasis is upon privacy and the deliberate effort on our part to be with the Father "who is there in the secret place."

Jesus knew that the ultimate struggle takes place in the private recesses of the self. Our wrestling with "principalities" and "powers" (see Eph. 6:12, RSV) may indeed become a social or political battle. But we never get to that battle and *stay with it* unless we engage in the struggle within.

Yesterday we thought about prayer as relationship. We learned that we choose our name for God by what God means to us. In Jesus' wisdom, he knew that our nature is such that when we are with others, with the exception of those we love and trust most, we are tempted to pretend to be less than honest, to play to our audience. When we are alone, we don't need to pretend. So we must go further to say that not only do we name God as God is for us; we name ourselves as *we* are before God.

The American Baptist Evangelism Team has suggested a model that deals with personal decision for Jesus Christ, which also assists us in naming ourselves as we are before God.

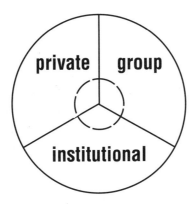

In the illustration above, the person is the dotted line at the intersection of the private/group/institutional arenas. Personal decision for Jesus Christ, therefore, means accepting him in the totality of one's private life, into one's groups (particularly family), and into one's institutional roles (as citizen or worker).

Our relationship to God is tremendously affected by the institutional and group realities of our existence. What we are as a citizen or worker, what we are as mother or father, son or daughter, what we are as a member of a political party or civic club are powerful dimensions of the self we are as we come to God in prayer.

God cannot and does not relate to what we are not. I don't mean that God can't break in upon our lives in any fashion and at any time God chooses. God does cut through our falseness, our counterfeit personalities, to bring us to judgment about our deception. Yet a living prayer relationship with God comes when we dare to *level* with God. When someone will not allow you beyond the very superficial levels of his or her life, there is little or nothing you can say. You only make "small talk." Likewise, when we present only a fictitious personality to God, when we pretend something we aren't, there is no real *presence* with which God can be truly present.

Reflecting and Recording

You have closed your prayer closet door now. God wants to be present with the real you. In God's presence now, look at yourself and name yourself. You, like I, probably have many names. You are legion: giant and weakling, hero and coward, laughter and cryer, reconciler and fighter, lover and hater, listener and talker, self-giving and selfish, sinner and saint. All the dimensions of the inner self are expressed in the private, group, and institutional arenas.

Spend some time naming yourself alone before God. Record five or six expressions of the legion you are.

1.
2.
3.
4.
5.
6.

Many of these expressions of ourselves are determined by the institutional, group, and private sectors of our living. Look back at the names you gave yourself a moment ago. Look at each one and make a note beside it of the sector (private, group, institution) that influences this expression of your being.

■ ■ ■

When we dedicate ourselves to God, God accepts us as we are. We need, therefore, to give our total selves to God—the good and bad, the positive and the negative.

Pray something like this as you close this period:

God, you are *my* God. Thank you for this time alone. I would like to have your presence as vivid as this throughout the whole day. Help me to know that you are with me, in whatever arena I find myself, even as I am, and that your strength can be my strength. And God bless (write below first names of those with whom you are sharing this adventure).

May they be strengthened by your presence.

Amen.

During the Day

Create some minutes within your routine today to recall this time when you were in solitude with God.

DAY TWO

"When You Pray, Do Not Be Like the Hypocrites"

Luke 18:10-14, PHILLIPS

Two men went up to the temple to pray, one a Pharisee and the other a tax collector. The Pharisee, standing by himself, was praying thus, "God, I thank you that I am not like other people: thieves, rogues, adulterers, or even like this tax collector. I fast twice a week; I give a tenth of all my income." But the tax collector, standing far off, would not even look up to heaven, but was beating his breast and saying, "God, be merciful to me, a sinner!" I tell you, this man went down to his home justified rather than the other; for all who exalt themselves will be humbled, but all who humble themselves will be exalted.

The eminent theologian John Cobb confessed the following:

I am driven back to this concern with prayer because I find no other way to achieve adequate self-knowledge, self-control, and stability of commitment. In the ordinary course of events I am not moved to careful and honest self-analysis. When I engage in self-examination in the presence of other persons, I cannot free myself from concern as to what they think of me or of what the consequences of my confession may be. When I seek professional help, I find that the categories through which I am helped to self-understanding deal only with limited aspects of my total being. In church when I join with others in confessing my sins, those sins are too generally stated to force me to more careful self-awareness. It is when I am alone that I can bring all these things together and go beyond them. But if I think of myself as simply alone, I do not find myself drawn to such painful analysis. As long as I am getting by with others, why should I judge myself more exactly than they do? It is only when I think of myself as being alone before God that traditional Christian self-examination, confession, and repentance make sense to me.[3]

Jesus taught us, "When you pray, do not be like the hypocrites; they love to say their prayers standing up in synagogue and at the street-corners for everyone to see them. I tell you this: they have their reward already. But when you pray, go into a room by yourself, shut the door, and pray to your Father who is there in the secret place; and your Father who sees what is secret will reward you" (Matt. 6:5-6, NEB).

Reflecting and Recording

Let's go further with the process we started yesterday—naming ourselves before God. Here is a framework for it.

1. *Self-examination.* Take a long, hard look at yourself. Don't pass over this quickly. Go beneath the surface. Spend five or ten minutes naming yourself as you are before God. Make some notes for only you to see.

2. *Confession.* Out of your self-examination did you become aware of some action or attitude, some hurtful relationship, some estrangement that you need to confess? In accepting ourselves, we do not accept indiscriminately those things that hinder our relationship with God and others. Confession is the way we clarify the

vision of who we are before God by acknowledging our destructive habits and seeking the *realignment* of our energies in more constructive directions. In accepting us, God takes even our sin and, through our confession, renders the misaligned intention behind it useful and productive! Write your confession here in a simple way.

3. *Repentance.* Repentance is the next step beyond confession. Some people confess without repentance. To repent is to be genuinely sorry for and pained by your sin. It is sincerely to turn away from it to seek a new life. If you do not feel genuinely sorry for or pained by your sin, ask God at this time to sensitize you to what you believe to be your sin, guiding you into constructive ways of dealing with it. You may later come to feel genuine repentance, or you may come to find what you believed was sin was really only a self-assigned guilt. Either way, it is a serious matter that needs to be revealed and abandoned under God's forgiving acceptance. When you are ready to take this step of repentance, make this prayer your own.

Dear God, I repent of _____
_____. I leave this behind and accept your forgiveness. Forgive me, set me free, and enable me to lead a new life. Amen.

Read this scripture promise aloud: "If we confess our sins, he who is faithful and just will forgive us our sins and cleanse us from all unrighteousness" (1 John 1:9).

Say a few words of thanks for God's forgiving love, accept God's forgiveness, and go in the freedom of it.

During the Day

Be attentive to your relationships with others today. See if you can catch yourself playing games with them, pretending to be something you aren't. When you catch yourself in pretense, quietly confess this to God and ask for help to be yourself.

DAY THREE

"When You Pray Don't Rattle Off Long Prayers"

Matthew 6:5-8, PHILLIPS

And then, when you pray, don't be like the play-actors. They love to stand and pray in the synagogues and at street-corners so that people may see them at it. Believe me, they have had all the reward they are going to get. But when you pray, go into your own room, shut your door and pray to your Father privately. Your Father who sees all private things will reward you. And when you pray don't rattle off long prayers like the pagans who think they will be heard because they use so many words. Don't be like them. For your Father knows your needs before you ask.

Thomas Moore saw seclusion as a kind of spiritual greenroom to which actors returned in their hired garments from the heat and public display of the stage. Jesus urged us not to be "like the play-actors" who pray to impress others. Prayer is relationship. It is primarily communication between one person and God.

Two days ago we made the distinction between simply being alone and being alone *with God*. We are not necessarily better persons when we are alone, only more genuine perhaps. The result of being alone and naming ourselves before God is that we can level about ourselves with God *and* with others. Thus solitude is preparation for more honest relationship and more deliberate participation with others and the world. So Jesus insists that our growth in prayer, our growth in relationship to the Father, is dependent upon that time alone with God.

In our aloneness with God, Jesus says, "Don't rattle off long prayers like the pagans who think they will be heard because they use so many words." In the world that Jesus knew, the gods of the people were remote, unpredictable, far removed from the affairs of earth. Prayer for the most part, in much of the religious practice of that day, was the effort on the part of an individual to win attention. So one made a lot of noise, rattled on and on. Such is not necessary; in fact, Jesus said it's repulsive to God. God is near—as near as breathing. God hears our longings even before we put them into words. God "knows your needs before you ask."

This does not mean that Jesus was against using words in prayer. Nor was he against asking God to meet our needs. On many occasions he poured his long-ings out to God and petitioned God in specific terms. Here Jesus is making the important point that it is not God who has removed God's self from us, but we who have removed ourselves from God.

The nearness of God, if we have the grace to grasp it, will transform our praying and our living. God's nearness makes all conversation with God intimate.

That means prayer can be a renewing and strengthening experience. When we are honest, most of us will admit that we are not nearly as strong as we sometimes think we are and often pretend to be. A word of ridicule, the turning away of a friend, an unexpected illness, even minor failures—not to mention *big* failures and tragic happenings—shatter our confidence. This happens even to practicing Christians. We think our confidence in God is great enough to keep us strong in faith and commitment, but these threats to our security explode the thought that we are mature in our faith.

So we come to God regularly, not to "rattle off long prayers" but to spend time in reflection, simply to be alone with God and to gain perspective for living.

Reflecting and Recording

1. Look back over the past week. Have there been times when your confidence was shattered? Were there times when you realized that you were not as strong as you pretended to be? Did you share that experience with anyone? Did you deliberately share it with God?

■ ■ ■

2. Do you know yourself as accepted as you are, rather than through the actions you perform or the masks you wear? Name three persons who accept you as you *really* are.

3. When the levels of human support fail, do you believe that God does actually sustain you, that God does provide strength? Recall two experiences when you felt God's strength vividly in your life. Record those experiences briefly here.

Here is a great promise upon which we can depend.

Isaiah 40:31

Those who wait for the LORD shall renew their strength,
    they shall mount up with wings like eagles,
they shall run and not be weary,
    they shall walk and not faint.

In my prayer life I find it meaningful to memorize such beautiful passages. You may also find such a practice meaningful. If so, memorize this verse or concentrate on it as you deliberately wait in silence for a few minutes for God to give you perspective and strength for the day ahead.

During the Day

Think now of the most difficult situation you might encounter today. It may be a task to perform, a personal encounter you anticipate, a decision you must make. Say *aloud* now, "God will be with me in that situation. No matter what happens, God is going to sustain me." When you approach that situation, remind yourself of this fact and remember the promise of the verse upon which you have been meditating: "Those who wait for the LORD. . . ." (This verse is printed on page 179. You may wish to clip it and carry it with you so that you may refer to it often.)

DAY FOUR

"When You Pray . . . Your Father Who Sees What Is Secret Will Reward You"

Isaiah 40:27-31

Why do you say, O Jacob, and speak, O Israel,
"My way is hidden from the LORD, and my right
    is disregarded by my God"?
Have you not known? Have you not heard?
The LORD is the everlasting God,
    the Creator of the ends of the earth.
He does not faint or grow weary;
    his understanding is unsearchable.

He gives power to the faint,
  and strengthens the powerless.
Even youths will faint and be weary;
  and the young will fall exhausted;
but those who wait for the LORD shall renew their strength,
  they shall mount up with wings like eagles,
they shall run and not be weary,
  they shall walk and not faint.

Did you carry that promise with you yesterday? What about your most difficult situation? Did you feel any different going through it, and after it was over? Spend a minute or two thinking about whether spending time alone with God prior to such an experience makes any difference.

■ ■ ■

Jesus said, "When you pray . . . shut your door and pray to your Father privately. Your Father who sees all private things will reward you." To be alone with God is necessary because, as we considered yesterday, we do need strength that is not our own. Our own strength and other human support is not enough. When we fail, when we don't make it or are turned off by others, we need to know that there is *Another* who can survive humiliation and failure and can help us survive.

In your recording yesterday, you listed two experiences when you felt God's strength vividly in your life. The truth is, there have been many experiences when such strength was not vivid. Isn't it true that the degree to which we feel God's presence and power in the daily affairs of life depends upon the degree to which we share with God *alone* in our "private room" or in the private company of our prayer group or partner?

As we grow in our prayer life, we will come to experience more and more what Jesus meant when he said that the Father "will reward you." Certainly we realize that we do not pray in order to be rewarded. We also realize that God does not play favorites and reward the righteous while abandoning the lost. In fact, the story of Job tells us that often the righteous fare much worse than the sinners. We learn the same from the cross! Perhaps we will be better off to consider the "rewards" of prayer as the natural consequences of praying. Just as every other act has its consequences, so does the act of prayer. So plant this fact firmly in your mind and heart: *The God with whom we can communicate is capable of answering our prayers.*

The writer to the Hebrews encourages us here: "Whoever would approach [God] must believe that he exists and that he rewards those who seek him" (Heb. 11:6).

At this early stage of our journey in prayer, three consequences need to be acknowledged and emphasized.

1. The consequence (reward) of God's *presence.* God is always present, but the end of all praying is to know the presence of God within our lives. All sorts of consequences flow from this greatest of all gifts of God.

2. The consequence (reward) of *power*. Our emphasis yesterday was on this fact: God makes a power not our own available to us.

3. The consequence (reward) of *guidance*. Prayer, being alone with God, opens our lives to the guidance of God. By its very nature, prayer encourages a *receptive mood*.

François Fénelon, one of the spiritual giants of all centuries, has written a prayer that will assist you in waiting in your secret place for the God who will reward you openly.

> Lord, I know not what I ought to ask of Thee; Thou only knowest what I need; Thou lovest me better than I know how to love myself. O Father! give to Thy child that which he himself knows not how to ask. I dare not ask either for crosses or consolations: I simply present myself before Thee, I open my heart to Thee. Behold my needs, which I know not myself; see and do according to Thy tender mercy. Smite, or heal; depress me, or raise me up: I adore all Thy purposes without knowing them; I am silent; I offer myself in sacrifice: I yield myself to Thee; I would have no other desire than to accomplish Thy will. Teach me to pray. Thyself in me. Amen.[4]

Reflecting and Recording

Fénelon's prayer is over two hundred years old. The language may be clumsy to you, but the *heart* of prayer is there. Go back over the prayer, slowly and deliberately. Then try to make it your own by rewriting it in your own words in this space.

During the Day

Dwell on this verse; embed the promise in your mind. "Whoever would approach [God] must believe that he exists and that he rewards those who seek him." This verse is printed on page 179. If you have not memorized it, you may wish to clip it and carry it with you today as a reminder that the consequences of your prayer relationship with God are God's *presence*, *power*, and *guidance*.

DAY FIVE

"Ask, and It Will Be Given You"

Matthew 7:7-11:

Ask, and it will be given you; search, and you will find; knock, and the door will be opened for you. For everyone who asks receives, and everyone who searches finds, and for everyone who knocks, the door will be opened. Is there anyone among you who, if your child asks him for bread, will give a stone? Or if the child asks for a fish, will give a snake? If you then, who are evil, know how to give good gifts to your children, how much more will your Father in heaven give good things to those who ask him!

There is no more expansive declaration about prayer than these words of Jesus confronting us in the Gospel of Matthew. Nothing could be bolder. All the resources of God are available to those who will enter into a praying relationship with God. Since this is such an extravagant promise, stop now and immerse yourself in verses seven and eight printed above. To memorize these verses will be meaningful to many.

■ ■ ■

Those who have barely entered the door of Christ's "school of prayer" may grab hold of this promise and begin to besiege the Father with all sorts of requests. That's OK, provided we don't reduce God to some sort of cosmic Santa Claus who is at the beck and call of selfish children. I personally believe that we should talk to God about anything we *feel* is important to us. I believe we should petition God for any gift we *think* we need. Anything that is important to us is important to God. Talking to God about anything and everything helps us find our way to a life of prayer.

The important thing is that we keep on talking with God, keep on bringing our desires and longings to God until we are clear in our own thinking about our needs. God does not grant us our wish-list. However, God does meet our needs and fulfill our longings.

The power of the promise, "Ask, and it will be given you," lies in the loving relationship between us as children and God as our Father. When we live in that relationship, we learn the spirit of the Father, we come to know his will, we act as a part of the family (the kingdom), we seek and find. So Jesus added that second word: "Is there anyone among you who, if your child asks for bread, will give a stone? Or if the child asks for a fish, will give a snake? If you then, who are evil, know how to give good gifts to your children, how much more will your Father in heaven give good things to those who ask him!" (Matt. 7:9-11).

We need to get firmly in our minds now the truly expansive power available through a prayer-relationship with God. As we grow in the relationship, we will understand the conditions and boundaries that guide our use of God's power (we don't seek to use this prayer power in ways God wouldn't use it). We will then begin to comprehend the wisdom of God in what appears to be unanswered prayer.

Here's what the gospel challenges us to recognize: Don't underestimate the power of God that comes to us through prayer. Don't set arbitrary limits on God. Don't box God in to the confines of present knowledge and imagination. Let God be God! Let God determine the boundaries. (For example, God has set some boundaries in making you a free creature, capable of acting for or against God.) Remember, "how much more [than we can comprehend with our human experience and reasoning] will your Father . . . give good things to those who ask him!"

The big meaning here is that too often we add more limits to prayer than God does. God's answers to prayer are always better than our asking, and God is always more ready to hear than we are to pray.

Reflecting and Recording

1. What are the three boldest requests you ever made to God? Record them here.

     1.

     2.

     3.

2. Look back at those requests and ask yourself these questions:

a. Did you really believe that your requests would be granted?

b. Were they?

c. Were these bold requests consistent with what you believe God would want for you?

d. What happened in your life as a result of your having received or not having received your requests?

Stay with this examination of your bold prayer requests for five or ten minutes.

■ ■ ■

3. Now list the three boldest requests you would like to make of God today. You don't have to share these with anyone. They are your private property. Be honest and be free.

1.

2.

3.

In closing, pray a prayer like this: "Lord, I'm trying to believe your great promise. I don't know all that it means or how it can operate in my life; but I believe in you and that your will for me is good. Help me to begin to accept for myself, this very moment, all that you are seeking to give me. Amen."

During the Day

You may have memorized the extravagant promise of Jesus recorded in Matthew 7:7-8. Take it with you during the day. (It is printed on page 179 for you to clip and carry with you.) Repeat it often. Call it to mind especially when you may be confronted with difficulty and a need to pray.

DAY SIX

"If You Have Faith the Size of a Mustard Seed. . . "

Matthew 17:20

If you have faith the size of a mustard seed, you will say to this mountain, "Move from here to there," and it will move; and nothing will be impossible for you.

Both Mark (11:23) and Luke (17:5-6) record similar sayings of Jesus about "faith the size of a mustard seed." This word is as expansive and as extravagant as the one we considered yesterday: "Ask, and it will be given you; search, and you will find; knock, and the door will be opened for you. For everyone who asks receives, and everyone who searches finds, and for everyone who knocks, the door will be opened."

Obviously, Jesus is emphasizing *faith*. Faith is one of the chief elements required to mobilize the answer to our prayers. The New Testament is filled with this emphasis of Jesus.

Matthew 9:22

Your faith has made you well.

Matthew 15:28

Woman, great is your faith! Let it be done for you as you wish.

Mark 5:34

Daughter, your faith has made you well; go in peace, and be healed of your disease.

Mark 10:52

Jesus said to him, "Go; your faith has made you well." Immediately he regained his sight and followed him on the way.

Luke 7:50

And he said to the woman, "Your faith has saved you; go in peace."

On one occasion we hear the disciples asking Jesus why their prayers had been ineffective, and Jesus says plainly, "Because of your little faith" (Matt. 17:20). Jesus attributed the failure of his power in his own country to the people's unbelief (Matt. 13:58). Here is a rather startling thought to consider: Jesus put emphasis upon our faith as the condition of appropriating God's love and power. God's love and power are always there unconditionally, but faith receives them and puts them to work.

Here is that emphasis in Jesus' boldest expression. "If you have faith the size of a mustard seed, you will say to this mountain, 'Move from here to there,' and it will move; and nothing will be impossible for you." Concede, if you wish, that Jesus was speaking poetically as he often did, and that the moving of a mountain was not to be taken literally. Even so, the truth is there. I like the way Lewis Maclachlan put it.

If we understood the mountains to be mountains of difficulty or of temptation, or barriers to liberty, this striking figure of speech must be allowed its due significance. At the least Jesus is saying that very great hindrances can be removed by faith, that faith is a power that can take up quite insurmountable obstacles and lift them from our path, that it can change the whole landscape for us, that it can make possible what looks impossible. If this is a metaphor it is a big metaphor, and must have a big meaning.[5]

Reflecting and Recording

We need to remember, as we stated yesterday, that too often we impose more limits on prayer than God does. God's answers to prayer are always better than our asking. God is always more ready to hear than we are to pray.

The bold promise of Jesus considered yesterday, along with this equally bold affirmation today, must be considered in the context of the total message of Jesus concerning our relationship to God. To be in a relationship of faith that results in answered prayer is to be willing to entrust ourselves to God, to give ourselves to God's will for our lives, to put ourselves in God's care, to follow God's guidance in all the affairs of our lives.

When this kind of trusting faith is the soil out of which our praying grows, mountains will be moved. In light of the understanding of faith, look again at the two sets of bold requests you have made—those of the past and those you recorded yesterday. Is there a difference in the two lists? How did the requests on your first list fit into your ongoing trusting commitment to God? What about the second list, the boldest requests you are making of God in the present? Do they fit into a trusting relationship and commitment to God? Spend four or five minutes examining your requests in light of these questions.

■ ■ ■

Having thought about these last questions for a few minutes, write a brief prayer expressing where you are right now in relation to God. Ask God to make you bolder in your trusting and in your prayers.

During the Day

Since praying and trusting God are inseparable, be especially attentive to how you relate your life to God today. Are you going it alone? Are you calling on God just in times of desperation? Are you worrying about things that you should commit to God? Are you making decisions without thought of God's will? Especially ask these questions in relation to your *group* and the *institutional* roles that you examined on Day One of this week.

DAY SEVEN

"If Two of You Agree. . . . "

Prayer is one of the primary ways through which the power of God is set loose in the world and in our individual lives. Jesus was bold in his affirmation of the unlimited possibilities that are ours through faith. I hope that our minds are expanding to claim the promises Jesus offered.

Matthew 7:7-8

Ask, and it will be given you; search, and you will find; knock, and the door will be opened for you. For everyone who asks receives, and everyone who searches finds, and for everyone who knocks, the door will be opened.

Matthew 17:20

If you have faith the size of a mustard seed, you will say to this mountain, "Move from here to there," and it will move; and nothing will be impossible for you.

Of course, we can't get our minds around such expansive promises in a short time. What excitement will be added to our praying when we pray even out of a *longing* to appropriate this expansive faith!

So, while your mind is yet staggered by these promises, here is still more good news from Jesus:

Matthew 18:19-20

If two of you agree on earth about anything you ask, it will be done for you by my Father in heaven. For where two or three are gathered in my name, I am there among them.

Here is a dimension of prayer that we have not yet considered in this adventure: *praying with others.* Jesus was insistent that we find solitude and be alone with God. Here he is saying that the mind and will of God come to us when we pray with others.

"If two of you agree on earth about anything you ask, it will be done for you by my Father in heaven." Doesn't that boggle your mind? The implication here that we need to concentrate upon is *the focus that can come to our praying when we share with another or with a group.* Many times when we pray alone, it is difficult to sift our selfish desires from our real needs, difficult to keep clear our seeking the will of God rather than our own wills. Our overwhelming desires need to be examined, even somewhat suspiciously, lest they conflict with the fundamental desires of the heart. It is only the satisfaction of the deepest desires of the human heart which can bring fulfillment.

So we pray with another or a group, to test ourselves as it were, to get help in sifting through and sorting out the longings and desires that clamor for satisfaction and fulfillment.

The testing comes at two levels. One, it presses us to clarify our longings and desires. Two, it enables us to examine whether our deepest desires are good for us and are in keeping with God's will. The psalmist said, God "gave them their request; but sent leanness into their soul" (Psalm 106:15, KJV). Our desires are not always pure, certainly not always good for us. So we test them with others we trust.

Our praying, especially with another or a group, is a testing of the needs and longings we feel. Are your desires so deep, so important, maybe even so desperate, that you would like to find a prayer partner to *agree* with you in making specific petitions to God?

Who will that partner be? If your spouse is sharing this adventure, he or she should be your partner. If your spouse is not sharing this adventure, you probably will want to find someone who is. If you are not related to a group in this adventure, find a trusted person: pastor, wife, husband, or friend. Share this bold promise of Christ with that person, and how you are seeking to find guidance in your praying. Be confident that Christ will honor the promise to be present with you, and that God will answer your prayer.

Right now, pray for guidance in selecting that person.

■ ■ ■

When you have decided (and you don't have to decide right now), make plans to be with that person as soon as possible in order to share this prayer experience. When that happens, come back to this space and record your feelings.

During the Day

Each day many of us have brief meetings with persons with whom we can share what is going on in our lives. Today when you encounter such a person, tell him or her about this adventure in prayer. Share this intriguing promise of Jesus: "Where two or three are gathered in my name, I am there among them." Ask for his or her understanding and belief. Consider how this verse could affect your lives together.

If you do not meet a person with whom you can be that specific, perhaps you will find someone with whom you can share something like this: "John/Jane, I'm doing an experiment in prayer. . . ." Tell them something about it, then ask something like, "What do you think about prayer? Have you had any experience that would be helpful to me?" Let the conversation go where it will without its being an embarrassment to, or pressure upon, anyone.

Group Meeting
for Week Two

Introduction

Needs for group work: one three-by-five-inch index card for each person in the group

Participation in a group such as this is a covenant relationship. You will profit most as you keep the daily discipline of the twenty to thirty-minute period and as you faithfully attend these weekly meetings. Do not feel guilty if you have to miss a day or be discouraged even if you are unable to give the full twenty to thirty minutes in daily discipline. Don't hesitate sharing that with the group. We may learn something about ourselves as we share. We may discover, for instance, that we are unconsciously afraid of spending that daily time "alone with God" because of what God may reveal to us or require of us.

A lot of our growth hinges upon our group participation, so share as openly and honestly as you can. Listen to what persons are saying. If you are attentive, you may be able to pick up meaning beyond the surface of their words.

To be sensitive in this fashion is crucial. To respond immediately to the feelings we pick up is also crucial. Sometimes it is important for the group to focus its entire attention upon a particular individual. If some need or concern is expressed, it may be appropriate for the leader to ask the group to enter into a brief period of special prayer for the person or concerns revealed. Participants should not always depend upon the leader for this kind of sensitivity. The leader may miss it. Even if you aren't the leader, don't hesitate to ask the group to join you in special prayer. This praying may be silent, or some person may wish to lead the group in prayer.

Remember, you have a contribution to make to the group. What you consider trivial or unimportant may be just what another person needs to hear. We are not seeking to be profound but simply to share our experience.

Sharing Together

1. Again you may wish to begin your time together by each person's sharing the most meaningful day in this week's adventure.

2. Now share the most difficult day and why.

3. On Day Three you were asked to recall two experiences when you were keenly aware of God's strength in your life. Let each person share one of these experiences with the group.

4. Does it make any difference that you are spending time alone with God? What difference? Some persons in the group may have anticipated a difficult experience and prepared for that experience by being alone with God. If so, let them share that with the group.

5. On Days One and Two of this week, you focused on "naming" yourself before God. Did you find any major difference between what you are in the three different arenas of your life: private, group, institutional? Discuss how the practice of prayer may make you "one," and how wrestling with principalities and powers in your inner self, alone with God, may equip you to be a responsible person in all the arenas of your life.

6. On Day Four you centered on the consequences (rewards) of prayer: presence, power, guidance. Let each person share a fresh insight about the meaning of prayer received from this emphasis.

7. You were asked to tell some person about this prayer adventure. Let persons share the result of that experience with the group.

Praying Together

On Day Two of this week you were asked to name each person in your group in prayer. An important part of this six-week group adventure is the members' praying for one another daily. During these sharing sessions, you may wish to make some notes that will help you recall specific concerns related to each individual. These notes will assist you in praying for these concerns in a focused way.

1. In his "faith the size of a mustard seed" affirmation, Jesus emphasized our faith as the condition of appropriating God's love and power (Day Six). That love and power is always there unconditionally, but faith receives it and puts it to work.
    a. Reread Lewis Maclachlan's commentary on this passage (page 56). Let each person in the group now record on the three-by-five-inch index card the mountain with which he or she is struggling. Note this clearly enough that the group may know what the mountain is, without naming yourself.
    b. When all have finished recording, the leader will collect the cards, shuffle them, and then give one back to each person.
    c. Let each person read the card he or she now has and pray silently for the removal of that mountain.
    d. Now let each person read aloud what is recorded on the card, the group pausing in quiet prayer after each reading.

2. Now stand and join hands in a circle. Let the leader say something like this: "All of us face mountains. We may not know what one another's mountain is, but we know that faith moves mountains. We know that where two or three are gathered in Jesus' name, he is in the midst of us; and that if we agree together about anything we ask, God will do it.

"Let us then agree to two things: One, that each one of us will have the faith that will receive and put God's love and power to work. Two, that each one of our mountains will be removed or overcome, or that the mountain may actually become a *redemptive* part of our lives, making for a beautiful landscape." The leader may then offer a brief verbal prayer to close the meeting.

A Word of Encouragement

As you begin this third week of your journey, here are some thoughts to keep in mind.

Discipline is an important dimension of life, not slavish rigidity, but an ordering of life that enables you to be in control of your circumstances, rather than controlled by them. For most people, a designated time of prayer is essential for building a life of prayer.

If you have not yet established a regular time for your prayer period, try to find the right time for you this week. Experiment in the morning, after work, during the lunch hour, before retiring—find the time that seems best for you.

If you discover that you can't cover all the material and exercises given for a day, don't berate yourself. Get what you can out of what you do. There is no point in rushing over three or four steps of principles if you cannot or will not think deeply. Pray seriously about them one by one.

Don't hesitate to make decisions and resolves, but don't condemn yourself when you fail. God is patient and wants us to be patient with ourselves.

Intellectual assent to a great principle or possibility is important, but it does us little good until we act upon it.

Week Three

When All Else Fails, Follow Directions

INTRODUCTION
WEEK THREE

Revisiting the Title "Father"

On a number of days during the past two weeks, the image of God as Father has been emphasized. The Lord's Prayer, with which we are going to live this week, begins with the designation, "Our Father."

Perhaps this is a good time to discuss the father image of God in the Bible and in Christian liturgy, tradition, faith, and practice in light of the impact of feminist theology. The image of God as Father is by far the most dominant and frequently used in the New Testament.

Many Christians and Jews recognize that biblical language about God is pervasively figurative. That doesn't mean we can change these figures as we please because, as Roland M. Frye reminds us, biblical figures of speech typically serve as figures of thought and understanding (*Speaking the Christian God*). By distinguishing between similes and metaphors in the Bible, Frye also helps us understand why father remains many Christians' primary designation for God. According to Frye, similes compare: The Lord is "like an eagle that stirs up its nest, that flutters over its young" (Deut. 32:11, RSV). Another instance comes in Isaiah 66:13, where the Lord offers reassuring maternal compassion: "As a mother comforts her child, so I will comfort you; you shall be comforted in Jerusalem." Throughout scripture you have that kind of simile, where God is described as being *like* a rock, a bird, a mother hen, a spring in the desert, a shadow beneath a mighty rock.

Metaphor, by contrast, goes beyond simile to identify or name, such as in Deuteronomy 32:6: "Is not [God] your father, who created you, who made you and established you?" Unlike the simile, which is simply an effort to help us understand what something is like, the metaphor goes further to stretch meaning and understanding—to go beyond or even against customary, literal meaning. The metaphor may even produce a new, overarching understanding that has not been present.

So when we call God *Father*, we are saying this is who God is. In the Hebrew Scriptures, the specific image of father is not so prominent as it became in the teaching of Jesus. For a good part of Israel's history, the name of God would never be upon the lips of a person. So, while God is designated *Father* eleven times in the Hebrew Scriptures, the name is never invoked as such in prayer. In the New Testament, Jesus describes God as *Father* over 170 times, and Jesus never prays to God by any title other than Father.

So we find a specific movement throughout the history of Israel down to the coming of Jesus—a movement from a God who is so holy, so wholly-other, so mysterious that God is not commonly named intimately in prayer. Thus, simile abounds. That far awayness of God, that separation and unfathomable mystery, begins to be dissolved. The move of the prophets of the Hebrew Scriptures toward more intimacy involves the designation of God as *Father*, however infrequent that might be. It reaches its climax in the New Testament with Jesus' praying to God as *Father*, and his teaching us to pray, "Our Father who art in heaven" (RSV).

The designation of God as *Father* has nothing to do with gender. God is not a sexual being. The use of the term *father* describes a relationship of shared love and fellowship in which the father pours out all his blessings upon all his children.

We bear in mind that the revelation is not of father manifested as God but of God manifested as father. If we remember that, the image can enhance not only our praying but our theological understanding and our total relationship to God.

DAY ONE

"This Is How You Should Pray. . . . "

Matthew 6:9-13, NEB

Our Father in heaven,
thy name be hallowed;
thy kingdom come,
thy will be done,
on earth as in heaven.
Give us today our daily bread.
Forgive us the wrong we have done,
as we have forgiven those who have wronged us.
And do not bring us to the test,
but save us from the evil one.

In Matthew's record of the Sermon on the Mount, Jesus closes his teaching on prayer by giving us a model. We call this the Lord's Prayer. In Christian worship this has become the most common corporate prayer, so much so that few of us pray it privately.

In Luke's Gospel, the Lord's Prayer is given in response to the disciple's request, "Lord, teach us to pray" (Luke 11:1). Jesus' response was, "When you pray, say: 'Father. . . .'" The prayer was really given as a guide for our *private* praying. When all else fails in prayer efforts, we do well to follow Jesus' directions.

Because the Lord's Prayer has become so common and is used so often in public worship, there is a danger that we have turned it into the "babbling of the Pharisees" against which Jesus warned us. Therefore, we are going to live with this model for an entire week. We want to immerse ourselves in the mood, spirit, style, and content of this prayer. When this happens, we will never be without a *way* to pray meaningfully.

This prayer, as a model, reaffirms what we considered on Day Seven of our first week: Prayer is relationship and relationship is personal. We are praying to a specific God whom Jesus calls *Father*. Jesus used this word out of his personal history and the history of Israel. Relationship with God always involves cleansing and purifying (holiness). The symbol of burning fire is often used as it is in Isaiah's experience with the "burning coal" in the temple (Isa. 6:6, RSV), to show this work of God in our lives.

Jesus knew the commandments that underscore the righteousness of God. God may allow us to live in unrighteousness, but the consequence of that is destruction. So God is seen as a "devouring" or "consuming" fire (Deut. 4:24; Heb. 12:29). In an ongoing prayer relationship with God, the demands of holiness and righteousness are always present.

We affirmed earlier that we need have no fear about coming to God honestly as we are. In relationship with God, change is not only possible, it is inevitable. As we give ourselves to God's lordship, we will respond to God's commandments. We will experience God's holiness and righteousness. Instead of being a comforting retreat from the world, prayer becomes a battleground where we wrestle with what it means to live God's life in the world—the causes that demand our allegiance, the issues deserving our energy, the persons needing God's healing love through us. This is the way Jesus modeled prayer.

Most people prefer the familiar rendering of the prayer found in the King James Version of Matthew. I deliberately used the *New English Bible* at the beginning to get us out of the familiar rut that may keep us from probing the depths of this great prayer.

Go back now and read that translation slowly for more meaning. Put a slash (/) after each thought, something like this: Our Father/in heaven/

■ ■ ■

Reflecting and Recording

Go back now and pick out two of the thoughts that mean the most to you today. List those and elaborate on their meaning to you as a personal prayer. (See the sample below.)

"Thy will be done"—Today, Lord, someone asked me to consider a certain job. I was flattered, but I just came to my present responsibility six months ago. I'm frustrated. I need your guidance. I want to do your will. Assist me in sifting through selfish desires, need for recognition, temptation to greater power, opportunity for service, fulfillment, and use of my talents and gifts in this total ministry of your church. Help me to decide quickly so my attention will be focused and all my energy devoted to my ministry.

Two Thoughts:

1.

2.

Stay with your two thoughts for four or five minutes, adding to what you have written if new meaning comes to you. Then say thank you to Christ for giving us this model.

During the Day

You can quote the Lord's Prayer in twenty seconds. Even such a twenty-second "breather" may be helpful. Today, however, be more deliberate. Rather than say this prayer, *pray* it! Select some three-minute breaks during the day, and go through the prayer slowly—aloud or in your mind—stopping to consider each movement of the prayer.

DAY TWO

"Our Father in Heaven"

Do you remember the two assumptions that we laid down on the third and fourth days of our adventure? One, the God to whom we pray is good. Two, communication with God is possible.

We can trace much of our failure at prayer back to our failure in appropriating these two truths. It is important to remember that the *goodness* of God includes the dimensions of *holiness* and *righteousness*, which were understood and experienced in the history of Israel. Jesus was living and sharing out of that history. His scripture was the Hebrew Scriptures.

"Father" as an image for God is present in the Hebrew Scriptures, but it is rare. Jesus uses the term *Father* in addressing God to imply intimate connection. So we begin with this: "Our Father." This means that the power to which prayer is addressed is personal.

"Our Father in heaven." We've taken that "in heaven" too literally. As Gerhard Ebeling said in preaching on this passage, "To proclaim God as the God who is near, as Jesus did, is to put an end to the idea of heaven as God's distant dwelling place. . . . It is not that where heaven is, there is God, but rather where God is, there is heaven."[6] To pray to the God who is "in heaven" is to pray to the God who is infinitely nearer to us than even we are to ourselves. We find God near in the depths of our being, in our mind, or spirit. So Jesus said to the woman at the well in Samaria, "God is spirit: and they that worship him must worship in spirit and truth" (John 4:24).

"Our Father in heaven." There are two facets in this address: "Father"—gracious, personal. "In heaven"—of the nearness of mind and spirit.

When we put these two facets together, we have a God who is gracious and good, concerned about each one of us. God is entirely personal in God's regard for us, yet transcends the limits of human personality.

This means again that God is good and that communication with God is possible. God is not only the Father of all; God is the God of Abraham, Isaac, Jacob, Maxie, and _____ (write your name in this blank). A father can love his family in general only by loving the several members in particular.

Once we come to believe this, the task of prayer is to lay hold on this experience by being cared for by our Father, communicating with God. Harry Emerson Fosdick reminds us that "belief by itself is a map of the unvisited land of God's care; prayer is actually traveling the country."

Reflecting and Recording

Because of individual experiences, some persons have difficulty with *father* as an image of God. We need to remember that for Jesus the revelation is not of the father manifested as God, but of God manifested as Father. Even so, instead of father, you may wish to think of the person within your relationships who has cared the most for you, the one who has been committed to assisting you in fulfilling your potential.

1. List eight attributes and actions that would describe the care of a father for his children, or the one who has loved you dearly.

a.

b.

c.

d.

e.

f.

g.

h.

Select four of these that would mean the most to you today.

a.

b.

c.

d.

2. God wants us to have what will mean the most to us today. Let's practice receiving what God has to offer. Get in a relaxed position. Sit with both feet on the floor. Rest your hands on your legs with your palms upward. Open your hands in a relaxed fashion and imagine that you are receiving gifts from God. Think of the first of the four attributes or actions that you listed as being the most meaningful

to you. In your open hands symbolically receive it as a gift from God and think about what it would mean to your life.

Now think of the second attribute or action of a caring father that you listed as most meaningful to you. Receive it in the same fashion. Now the third and finally the fourth. (Some of these gifts may be anticipated in the future. Even so, the symbolic receiving of them will make you open and receptive to God's Spirit within you.)

To travel in the country of God's care is to believe that God gives, and to receive God's care is an adventure of the soul in the practice of prayer.

During the Day

If the last part of the experience (open hands—receiving gifts) seemed superficial to you, go through the day *acting* as though God does care. Try to stay conscious of the fact that God wants to give you what you need. For this to happen, we have to be open to receive.

DAY THREE

"Thy Name Be Hallowed; Thy Kingdom Come"

Today we consider two movements in Jesus' direction for our praying. Both are related.

"Thy name be hallowed. . . . " Even though the word *hallowed* is a clumsy, archaic word, the phrase rolls off our lips so smoothly. "Hallowed be thy name" (KJV). We move over it so quickly and easily that we hardly ponder its meaning.

Jesus must have known that we start praying at the wrong place. How often do we move into prayer, centering immediately on our troubles, problems, anxieties, needs. Many times our praying simply is the exercise of brooding over our morbid situations. We ought to "brood" in the presence of God, but it may be no more than that—brooding—if we don't follow Jesus' direction.

It was no accident that Jesus instructed us: Pray then like this: "Our Father in heaven, thy name be hallowed."

We are beginning where we should begin, with God. Before we start asking God for anything and start telling God our troubles and sorrows and anxieties, we focus on God's glory, love, and living presence. In this movement, I hope that we will allow God's Spirit to pervade and influence our minds.

To *hallow* is to praise, and there is power in praise. We express our praise and gratitude for what God has done and for who God is. I find singing, even in my private praying, to be one of my most meaningful ways of praising God. (I'll talk more about this on Day Six of Week Six.) Also, to *hallow* is to make holy. By naming God as holy in prayer, we place ourselves in a position to experience the majesty, mystery, and powerful presence of God. This is very important, for without this experience we just add pious words to a distant deity. If we name and therefore experience God as holy, we sense God's hallowed, holy presence in the world.

Stop now and meditate upon that phrase, "Thy name be hallowed." Focus on God's glory, love, presence, power. Spend two or three minutes with these thoughts.

■ ■ ■

Having meditated upon the meaning of this phrase, rewrite this first part of the Lord's Prayer in language that you may use more commonly.

_____

(Your way of saying it)

"Thy name be hallowed" flows naturally into the second petition: "Thy kingdom come." Again our focus remains outside ourselves.

That's a far-flung dream, and who stops to consider what it really means? In a sense we have no choice about the coming of God's kingdom. It has already come in Jesus. Jesus began his public ministry with the announcement, "The time is fulfilled, and the kingdom of God has come near; repent, and believe in the good news" (Mark 1:15). He said to the Pharisees, "The kingdom of God is among you" (Luke 17:21). So in a sense, God's kingdom has already come.

We also need to recognize that we do not "build the kingdom." God *brings* the kingdom. God *gives* the kingdom. It is God's *design* and *doing*.

Even so, Jesus directs us to pray, "Thy kingdom come." He knew that what we focus our hearts and minds upon will become a reality in our lives. The King James Version of Proverbs 23:7 reminds us that as persons think, so they are.

The kingdom of God means the reigning activity of Christ in human hearts and society. So wherever Christ's rule or reigning activity is experienced (be it in peace, in human justice, in healing, in shared love, in reconciliation), there is the kingdom of God. To pray for this rule of Christ is a big petition—a huge desire. No wonder Jesus compared it to "the pearl of great price" or "the treasure hidden in a field."

Matthew 13:44-46

The kingdom of heaven is like treasure hidden in a field, which someone found and hid; then in his joy he goes and sells all that he has and buys that field.

Again, the kingdom of heaven is like a merchant in search of fine pearls; on finding one pearl of great value, he went and sold all that he had and bought it.

"Thy kingdom come." This is no prayer for anyone who does not want to change.

Reflecting and Recording

If the kingdom of God means the rule of Christ over human hearts and society, consider the changes that would have to take place for the kingdom to become a reality.

What changes would have to take place in your life for the rule of Christ to be dominant? These questions will help you in your reflection: What do you want more than anything else today? What is your *money situation* today? How are you spending your money? What have you been *worrying* most about this week? What do you *love* most? How do you spend the time you have apart from your job?

■ ■ ■

1. For your own reflection, be specific and write by each word listed the changes necessary for the kingdom to be realized in you.

Money

Time

What I love most

What I worry about

What about your community? The kingdom of God means the rule of Christ over society. What are the obvious areas of community life, social conditions, where the rule of Christ is not present?

2. "Thy kingdom come"—what are you willing to do to receive (or to gain or to realize) the "pearl of great price," the kingdom *for your own life?* (Record that commitment here.)

3. How are you going to put your prayer, "Thy kingdom come," to work in your community?

During the Day

You know by now that you don't settle the kinds of questions with which we've been dealing in a thirty-minute period. It's a lifetime proposition. For that reason we keep on praying, "Thy name be hallowed; thy kingdom come." Continue to reflect upon these meanings and beginnings throughout the day. In the persons and situations that you encounter today, ask yourself, "What does it mean for God's name to be hallowed here?" "What would it mean for God's kingdom to be fully realized in this situation and in this relationship?"

DAY FOUR

"Thy Will Be Done"

Matthew 26:36-46, PHILLIPS

Then Jesus came with the disciples to a place called Gethsemane and said to them, "Sit down here while I go over there and pray." Then he took with him Peter and the two sons of Zebedee and began to be in terrible pain and agony of mind. "My heart is breaking with a death-like grief," he told them, "stay here and keep watch with me." Then he walked on a little way and fell on his face and prayed, "My Father, if it is possible let this cup pass from me—yet it must not be what I want, but what you want."

Then he came back to the disciples and found them fast asleep. He spoke to Peter, "Couldn't you three keep awake with me for a single hour? Watch and pray, all of you, that you may not have to face temptation. Your spirit is willing, but human nature is weak."

Then he went away a second time and prayed, "My Father, if it is not possible for this cup to pass from me without my drinking it, then your will must be done." And he came and found them asleep again, for they could not keep their eyes open. So he left them and went away again and prayed for the third time using the same words as before. Then he came back to his disciples and spoke to them, "Are you still sleeping and taking your ease? In a moment you will see the Son of Man betrayed into the hands of evil [ones]. Wake up, let us be going! Look, here comes my betrayer!"

Jesus did not teach that God would give us anything and everything we asked. There are *genuine* limitations to what is granted in prayer. Last week we considered those bold, extravagant promises of Jesus:

Ask, and it will be given you;
Seek, and you will find;
Knock, and it will be opened to you. (RSV)
If you have faith the size of a mustard seed . . .
nothing will be impossible for you.
If two of you agree . . . it will be done.

We considered the conditions of those promises: living in a trusting relationship with God and asking in the spirit and under the guidance of Christ. Now comes the summary of all conditions: "Thy will be done."

God did not give Jesus everything he asked. Jesus wasn't playing at prayer in Gethsemane. The cross was looming ahead. This was the dark night of his soul, the ultimate struggle of his life. Read the story again (printed above), and try to put yourself in Jesus' place.

■ ■ ■

Three times Jesus repeated the petition. It was not a light, thoughtless, shallow "Lord, give me _____." He agonized over what was happening. So deep was his anguish that the Gospel writer says his face was stained with sweat drops of blood.

"Let this cup pass"—if it be possible deliver me from death. "No" was God's answer to that particular petition.

In the deepest agony of his life, Jesus prayed as he had taught his disciples to pray.

Matthew 6:9-10

Pray in this way: . . . Thy kingdom come. Thy will be done, on earth as in heaven."

Matthew 26:39, PHILLIPS

My Father, if it is possible let this cup pass from me—yet it must not be what I want, but what you want.

To pray as Jesus taught is to put ourselves in the center of God's will. There is no more important dimension of prayer than this.

To pray "thy will be done" is also an affirmation of God's call and our vocation. None of us is helpless, and the hopeless "what can I do" question does not fit into a life of prayer. In our prayer we often identify our gifts and hear God's call. To pray "thy will be done" is to say, "Here am I, send me!"

But there is something else in this particular teaching of Jesus. We will pass over it if we aren't careful. "Thy will be done, on earth as in heaven" is not so much a petition in the Lord's Prayer as it is a strong, emphatic assertion. When we pray this as Jesus taught us, we are making an affirmation. Such an affirmation can work wonders in our lives. We need to petition God, even as Jesus did, and make our requests known. But once we have done so, we should not dwell on our needs and desires. Rather, we should center upon the will of God being realized on earth—God willing to do for us "exceeding abundantly above all that we ask or think" (Eph. 3:20, KJV).

I find this assertion meaningful. There are only two legitimate positions for a Christian: kneeling in prayer saying, "Thy will be done"; or standing erect in readiness saying, "Here am I, send me."

Reflecting and Recording

1. Look again at the model of personhood presented on page 43. Institutionally we have become technological persons. We feel driven and hopelessly bound to the systems that determine our lives. But are we hopeless?

2. Look at your role as a worker or citizen. What are you doing that is destructive to your best self or to the good of other persons because you feel bound in the system? Record your conclusions here.

3. What will you do about that destructiveness? Be specific by writing down some specific effort you will put forth.

4. Look at the groups you are part of (such as family, club, political party). What does praying "thy will be done" have to do with these parts of your life?

(family) _____

(Group name) _____

(Group name) _____

During the Day

Throughout this day, stay conscious of what you have recorded during this time of reflection. As you approach your work and personal involvements, seek to make this prayer a reality: "Thy will be done."

DAY FIVE

"Give Us Today Our Daily Bread"

Luke 12:15-25

[Jesus] said to them, "Take care! Be on your guard against all kinds of greed; for one's life does not consist in the abundance of possessions." Then he told them a parable: "The land of a rich man produced abundantly. And he thought to himself, 'What should I do, for I have no place to store my crops?' Then he said, 'I will do this: I will pull down my barns and build larger ones, and there I will store all my grain and my goods. And I will say to my soul, "Soul, you have

ample goods laid up for many years; relax, eat, drink, be merry." But God said to him, 'You fool! This very night your life is being demanded of you. And the things you have prepared, whose will they be?' So it is with those who store up treasures for themselves but are not rich toward God." He said to his disciples, "Therefore I tell you, do not worry about your life, what you will eat, or about your body, what you will wear. For life is more than food, and the body more than clothing. Consider the ravens: they neither sow nor reap, they have neither storehouse nor barn, and yet God feeds them. Of how much more value are you than the birds! And can any of you by worrying add a single hour to your span of life?

The house of prayer is not a shop where we go to bargain and barter for the gifts of God. It is the home of the Father with whom we live, where all the treasures of God's love and concern are ours for the receiving.

"Give us today our daily bread." This is petition; it is asking God for the common needs of life. But more than petition, it is *commitment*. In the same setting where Matthew records the Lord's Prayer, he shares that assuring word of Jesus about all our needs being satisfied by the Father.

Matthew 6:25-26, Phillips

Don't worry about living—wondering what you are going to eat or drink, or what you are going to wear. Surely life is more important than food, and the body more important than the clothes you wear. Look at the birds in the sky. They never sow nor reap nor store away in barns, and yet your Heavenly Father feeds them. Aren't you much more valuable to [God] than they are?

In telling us to pray for the bread we need for today, yet at the same time not to worry about our eating and drinking, Jesus is saying all that we need to maintain our lives as gifts from God. We ought, therefore, to have no anxiety about them.

The dominant desires of our lives are the petitions of our prayers. For many of us our society has so intensified our desires that our prayer for daily bread has become the mark of our sinfulness. This is one of the lessons of the "rich fool." Desire has to be restrained.

This we must affirm over and over again: *God is the giver.* God gives us the things we need, or, as Luke puts it, God keeps on giving us day by day. This has tremendous implications for our lives, and especially for our praying. The accent is transferred from the life of effort to the life of faith. Many of us are able to affirm that we are utterly dependent upon God for the salvation of our souls, yet are unwilling to carry this commitment into the whole of life.

I am dependent upon God for all of life! Ponder this thought for a few minutes. What does it mean? Can you accept it? Do you live as though it were true?

Here is also a great understanding of *stewardship.* All that we have comes from God. God has provided enough resources for the needs of all people. We can live on this earth that has become a global village if the fortunate ones who have plenty to spare will be responsible stewards, will cease "tearing down their barns and building bigger barns," will let God determine their desires, rather than having them determined by the technology that makes us gluttonous consumers.

To believe that we are dependent upon God for our energy, for the air we breathe, for life itself, does not mean that we sit back and do nothing. Not to be anxious about tomorrow (what we are to eat, or drink, or wear) is not to diminish the meaning of our labor and the creative use of our talents. It is to dedicate all that we are to the Giver of life and to open ourselves to receive what God has to offer us and what God, through us, has to offer others.

In prayer, then, we receive from God by faith all that we need to meet the demands of life. So "give us today our daily bread" is more than a petition; it is a *commitment.* It is saying to God: "Everything I need comes from you. I am open to receive it. I face this day and all of life believing that you will supply all my needs."

When we believe that our very life is God's gift and when we act in response to that belief, then we will stay in touch with reality and with the source of reality, which is God.

Reflecting and Recording

It helps us to be specific about our needs and to bring them to God. Obviously Jesus thought it was important to pray even for daily bread. Record your primary needs for today in these blanks as designated.

Physical and Material Needs	Spiritual and Emotional Needs
_____	_____
_____	_____
_____	_____
_____	_____
_____	_____

It is only partially true that we propose and God disposes. God has already given us gifts in abundance. We are to use these gifts to meet our needs and the needs of others. Look at the list above. Are there any needs to which God has already responded by giving you the resources and talents to meet those needs? If so, commit yourself to releasing what resources you have for meeting those needs. Pray for guidance in using the gifts God has already given you.

There are needs in your list for which you seem to have no resources. Make a new list, designating those in the space below. You don't have to put them into categories.

Now will you pray something like this: "Lord Jesus, you've told me to pray today for the bread I need. You've told me not to be anxious, though, about what

I'm going to eat or drink or wear. You've assured me that if an earthly father knows how to give good gifts to his children, my heavenly Father will give even more abundantly than I can ask or think. So here are what I think my needs are (list them as recorded above). I leave these needs to your supply, and I open myself to receive whatever you have to offer, believing that what you have to offer is far greater even than the meeting of these needs. In that assurance I commit myself anew to your loving care today. Amen."

During the Day

God wants to meet the needs of all his children. God has given to some of us the gifts and resources to meet the needs of God's other children. Somewhere today a person whose path may cross yours prayed the same kind of prayer that you have prayed: a prayer for "daily bread," a prayer that God would meet his or her needs. You may be God's answer for that person. Be open to that possibility today and in the days ahead. Try to be sensitive to God's desire to work in your life to fill the needs of others. Name here one person who has a need you can meet: (_____). Do something today to begin to meet that need.

DAY SIX

"Forgive Us . . . As We Also Have Forgiven"

As you begin your adventure today, pray quietly but aloud, slowly, deliberately, the prayer Jesus taught us.

Matthew 6:9-13, RSV

Our Father who art in heaven,
Hallowed be thy name.
Thy kingdom come,
Thy will be done,
On earth as it is in heaven.
Give us this day our daily bread;
And forgive us our debts,
As we also have forgiven our debtors;
And lead us not into temptation,
But deliver us from evil.

The logic of the Lord's Prayer is so clear. We begin by focusing on God: "Our Father who art in heaven, hallowed be thy name." We continue by praying for the kingdom to come on "earth as it is in heaven." The focus is still on God but is more personal in terms of God's rule in our lives and in our community. It is "God's will" for which we are asking.

Then we pray for "bread," the very sustenance of life, believing that we are dependent upon God for all of life.

Now comes the prayer for pardon: "And forgive us our debts, as we also have forgiven our debtors." Notice the word *and*, linking the prayer for pardon with the request for bread. How clear the logic! Jesus knew that God offers two kinds of food: food for the body and food for the soul; one to sustain life, the other to make life free and whole.

Most translations of Matthew's version of the Lord's Prayer use the word *debts*, while in Luke's version they use the word *sins*. *The New English Bible* speaks of *wrongs*. *The Book of Common Prayer*, from which many pray in public worship, uses the word *trespasses*. All these translations are illuminating and interchangeable, providing different facets of the same truth.

Debts: Though we may think we are reasonably free from creditors or obligations to other people who have done us favors, we are nevertheless indebted to God for our very existence! The truth of the matter is that we live in a world of interdependency with others and with God. Our responsibilities toward neighbor and God form a network of debts. We owe so much more than we can ever repay that our humble prayer must be "forgive us our debts."

Sins or Wrongs: They are those things we have done that were morally wrong—the breaking of God's law.

Trespasses: To trespass means to go where we don't belong; to pass over land that isn't open to us; going against God, violating God's will; going against persons, violating their personal rights.

Whatever word we use, the truth is that no person can *pay* his or her debt to God, no person can forgive his or her own sins, no person can *make right* his or her trespasses. It is the very nature of forgiveness that it has to come from beyond us from another person or from God, from the one we have hurt, sinned against, from the one we have trespassed against, from the one we owe. Forgiveness has to come from beyond us, and it has to be given freely. We don't *pay* for it, but Jesus said we are to *pray* for it.

Sin is separation from God; forgiveness is reconciliation with God. The amazing truth of the gospel is that forgiveness is ours. "In Christ God was reconciling the world to himself" (2 Cor. 5:19).

To pray ought to mean that we open ourselves to receive the forgiveness of God. Again here is the truth we emphasized yesterday: God is the giver. The Father wants to give good gifts to his children. God wants us to receive the forgiveness offered.

Yet we don't. We remain separated from God because we will not receive God's gift of forgiveness. We want to *do* something to *earn* it. We want to *make things right ourselves.* So, in our struggles we remain separated.

Ponder this for a minute or two: *God has already forgiven you.*

■ ■ ■

The necessary movement on your part is to accept that forgiveness. Accepting God's forgiveness will lead us to repentance. So, overwhelmed by the love and acceptance of God, we will be truly sorry for our debts, our wrongs, our sins, our trespasses. Forgiveness brings repentance.

Accepting God's forgiveness will lead us to seek to *make right our wrongdoing.* We call it restitution. It will make us want to seek reconciliation with our neighbor. It will cause us to desire to rectify our past. Zacchaeus experienced this forgiveness and said, "Half of my possessions, Lord, I will give to the poor; and if I have defrauded anyone of anything, I will pay back four times as much" (Luke 19:8).

So Jesus ties two movements together: "Forgive us our debts, as we also have forgiven our debtors." Receiving forgiveness is dependent upon having a forgiving spirit. Could it be that this is the reason forgiveness is often unreal in our lives? We are unable to receive forgiveness because we do not have a forgiving spirit. We have not forgiven others. This was so important to Jesus that he stressed the truth in his parable of the two debtors (Matt. 18:21-35).

Peter asked Jesus, "Lord, if another member of the church sins against me, how often should I forgive?" Jesus responded, "Not seven times, but, I tell you, seventy-seven times." Then he told the parable of the two debtors. Out of the largeness of his heart, the king canceled the debt of one of his servants. This lucky servant then turned on a fellow-servant and demanded that a paltry sum be repaid. When it wasn't, rather than extending the kind of forgiveness he had experienced from the king, the forgiven servant had his fellow servant thrown into a debtor's prison. Hearing this news, the king reversed his judgment and threw the ungrateful servant into jail.

Jesus concluded that parable with this tough word: "So my heavenly Father will also do to every one of you, if you do not forgive your brother or sister from your heart" (Matt. 18:35).

There are wide-ranging implications here. Primarily though, Jesus is undergirding with this parable what he taught us about praying: "Forgive us our debts, as we also have forgiven our debtors."

Reflecting and Recording

1. Go back and reread what was said about those three facets of the same truth: *debts, sins* or *wrongs,* and *trespasses.* Be specific in confessing in the space below how they find expression in your life.

Debts:

Sins or *wrongs*:

Trespasses:

2. Forgiveness is a gift of God. We are open to receive it as we have a forgiving spirit. Are there persons who have wronged you whom you need to forgive? Who are they, and for what are you holding them *guilty?*

Forgiveness is a gift of God. Often God's forgiveness can be real in our lives only as we *forgive ourselves.* Are you carrying a burden of guilt because you have not yet forgiven yourself? Think about that. If it is true, admit it and say a prayer similar to this:

> Lord Jesus, I accept your forgiveness, but I confess that I have not forgiven myself. Today I forgive myself for (fill in the blank with whatever it is for which you need to forgive yourself) _____ _____. I know that you accept me. Now help me to accept myself. Don't let me fall back into self-condemnation again. Amen.

During the Day

You made a list of the persons you need to forgive, with whom you need to be reconciled. During this day at least begin the process of reconciliation—a phone call, an e-mail, a text, a letter, a personal contact, anything to show your "forgiving spirit"—so you can feel the freedom of forgiveness.

Last week in our emphasis on "if two of you shall agree," you were asked to find a prayer partner. You may want to talk to that person again about this need to forgive and be reconciled.

DAY SEVEN

"And Lead Us Not into Temptation, but Deliver Us from Evil"

Below is the Lord's Prayer as we commonly pray it in public worship. We have been living with this prayer for a week now. We are beginning really to make it our own. Write your own prayer, using your words and following this model, beside Jesus' instruction.

Pray then like this:

Our Father who art in heaven,

Hallowed be thy name.

Thy kingdom come,

Thy will be done,
On earth as it is in heaven.

Give us this day our daily bread;

And forgive us our debts,
As we also have forgiven our debtors;

And lead us not into temptation,
But deliver us from evil.

Jesus' logic continues to be clear in the Lord's Prayer. "Forgive us . . . as we forgive." We are forgiven—our mountainous debts that we owe to God; the wrongs that we have done; the sins we have committed in thought, word, and deed. With amazing grace, in unlimited mercy, God loves and forgives us, accepts us, and marks the account settled.

"And lead us not into temptation, but deliver us from evil." This follows naturally the petition to be forgiven. We not only need God's forgiveness for what has been; we need God's protection against what may come.

What a strange petition, "Lead us not into temptation"! Why should we have to ask God not to lead us into temptation? Certainly this prayer is more than a plea to be excused from the various trials and tempting opportunities that promise us life but grant us failure and abandonment. Christian life, as the cross shows us, is participation in and not exemption from the trials and tempting opportunities of life. This petition does not say "excuse us from life's temptations"; rather it is a plea that we shall not be abandoned during our wrestling with deceiving powers and opportunities. It is the feeling of abandonment and despair that makes temptation so fearful. So we pray not to be led into the ultimate consequence of temptation, that sense of having been "taken" and now abandoned. We are to claim Paul's promise that no tempting power, "neither death, nor life, . . . nor powers, . . . nor anything else in all creation, will be able to separate us from the love of God in Christ Jesus our Lord" (Rom. 8:38-39).

"But deliver us from evil." Like the petition "lead us not into temptation," this one is not a prayer for special treatment from God, as though God could prevent evil from going our way. Rather the petition is about handling the very real evil we all experience. We pray to be delivered, and that's not the same as being exempted from evil. Deliverance is liberation, being freed from the threat that evil can ultimately destroy us. Notice this: It is liberation for everyone, not just the faithful or the righteous—"Deliver *us*," not "Deliver those who pray or those who attend church regularly." Are we prepared to pray this petition seriously, to ask God for the deliverance and liberation of everyone, including those we may be oppressing and afflicting with evil (by indifference, greed, pride, or feelings of superiority)? What changes would we have to make in our lives and relations with others if we prayed this petition seriously?

Here is a dimension of prayer and Christian living that is missing from too many of our lives. Too often prayer becomes a response to what has been, rather than an experience of what is and what can be. In praying about temptation and liberation from evil, we look to the God who calls us forward to meet these challenges. We lay claim to the *living Christ* who is a continuing part of our experience and yet is ahead of us, encouraging us on.

Jesus invites us to give ourselves to him and to allow his matchless energy to be the power of our living.

John 15:1, 4-5

I am the true vine. . . . Abide in me as I abide in you. . . . You are the branches. Those who abide in me and I in them bear much fruit.

Our praying and our living will never be the vital vibrant experience that they can be until we grasp this. Abiding in Christ, allowing his spirit to live in us, is our source of power. Allowing his *life* to live in us, we pray, "Lead us not into temptation, but deliver us from evil."

The gospel is the good news of the Deliverer. The Deliverer is Christ. He is on our side in our struggle against any power that would tempt us to sin or would seek to destroy us. He is God's answer to our prayer, "Lead us not into temptation, but deliver us from evil."

Reflecting and Recording

Get the symbol of the vine and the branches in your mind. All the branches are linked to the vine. The branches depend upon the vine for life itself. The fruits upon the branches are brought to birth, fed, and brought to fulfillment (ripened) by the life that comes through the vine.

See yourself as a branch with Jesus as the vine, abiding in him and he in you. Write a prayer about what that means to you, and how you will seek to live it out.

During the Day

Some think it too simplistic to confront problems and temptations with the question, "What would Jesus do?" Yet guidance can come in that fashion. Perhaps a better way to think of it is this: "If I am truly a branch of his vine, if I am abiding in him and he in me, where should I go, what should I do, how should I respond today in this situation with this person?" Add to that the fact that abiding in him, his power becomes your power. Therefore you do not face problems and temptations alone.

Keep this vision in mind throughout the day. Stay aware or call to awareness the living, indwelling Christ as your Deliverer, as God's answer to your prayer: "Lead me not into temptation, but deliver me and all of us from the evil we inflict on one another."

Group Meeting for Week Three

Introduction

Needs for group work: chalkboard, whiteboard, or newsprint

Feedback is necessary to keep the group dynamic working positively for all participants. The leader should be sensitive to this. Persons should be encouraged to share their feelings about how the group is functioning. You may want to begin this session by asking for feedback.

Feedback is also essential for communication because we often mishear what a person is saying. A simple practice of feeding back to the person what you have heard (for example, "I hear you saying that you feel guilty because you have to *force* yourself to pray. Is that it?") will enhance communication.

This has significant meaning in prayer. We want to know that we are being heard. To be heard by our friends may be the first step in our experience of God as a friend who really hears! So each of us then should practice listening, also feeding back to check meaning in order that our fellow prayer-pilgrims may know that we really hear. It takes only one or two persons attempting this kind of serious listening to set the mood for the entire group.

Sharing Together

1. Did you experience anything fresh or different about praying the Lord's Prayer this week? Share this with the group.

2. The "during the day" suggestion for Day Five of this week was for you to be open to the possibility of being God's answer to someone's prayer for "daily bread." Let each person share his or her experience following that suggestion. Did such an opportunity arise? Did you respond? How did you feel about it?

3. Look at Day One of this week in your workbook. You divided the Lord's Prayer into single thoughts. Go through the prayer and select the thought you would *most willingly* omit from the prayer. Underline that phrase. (Take enough time to do this deliberately.)

a. Now let each person in the group share why he or she chose that particular phrase.

b. After all have shared, select a person to record on a chalkboard, whiteboard, or on newsprint new insights that have come to any person from this discussion.

Praying Together

Corporate prayer is one of the great blessings of Christian community. To affirm that is one thing; to experience it is another. To *experience* it we have to *experiment* with the possibility. While Jesus insisted that being alone with God is a basic dimension of prayer, we need to understand also the possibility of the mind and will of God becoming clear to us when we pray with others: "If two of you shall agree."

Will you become a bit bolder now and experiment with the possibilities of corporate prayer by sharing more openly and intimately?

1. In your "Reflecting and Recording" period of Day Three this week, you were asked to be specific in designating the changes necessary for the kingdom to be realized to you.

a. Spend three minutes in quietness now, reflecting again upon those necessary changes. Select one you are willing to share with the group members—that they may pray with you and for you.

b. Let each person share with the group one need for change. (Again it will be helpful if you make some notes to remind you during the week of the needs of your friends.)

2. There is a sense in which, through this sharing, you have already been praying corporately. There is power, however, in a community on a common journey

verbalizing thoughts and feelings to God in the presence of fellow pilgrims. Experiment with this possibility now.

a. Let the leader call each person's name, pausing briefly after each name for some person in the group to offer a brief verbal prayer focused on what that person has shared. It should be as simple as, "Lord, give Jane victory over her bitterness toward her neighbor." (Leader, remember to call your own name.)

b. When all names have been called, and all persons prayed for, sit in silence for two minutes; be open to the strength of love that is ours in community. Enjoy being linked with persons who are mutually concerned.

c. After this time of quietness the leader may simply close the meeting by saying, "Amen!"

Week Four

Basic Ingredients of Prayer and Discovering Your Pattern

INTRODUCTION
WEEK FOUR

Trusting the Lord to Provide the Future

Earlier I talked about an affirmation that served me well during my painful, wrenching transition. It came from the heart of God to me when I desperately needed it: "The will of God will never take us where the grace of God will not sustain us."

The Hebrew Scripture story of Abraham offering his son Isaac as a sacrifice to the Lord is one of the most dramatic stories in the Bible. It's not an easy story to understand or accept. Who can begin to identify with Abraham—when the Lord asks him to sacrifice his only son?

The story begins with this word: "After these things God tested Abraham," and there follows the story of the sacrifice of Isaac by Abraham.

When you read the Bible, especially the Hebrew Scriptures, the message seems to be that God *causes* everything to happen. There is no hesitation to accredit to God all the afflictions as well as the blessings of life. Here is a very frequent expression of this in the Hebrew Scriptures.

Psalm 66:10-12, NKJV

For you, O God, have tested us;
　　you have tried us as silver is tried.
You brought us into the net;
　　you laid burdens on our backs;
you let people ride over our heads;
　　we went through fire and through water;
yet you have brought us out to a spacious
　　place.

What we need to remember is that the Hebrew mind did not have the distinctive cause/effect approach to experience. It did not make a distinction between God's *causing* and God's *allowing*. The Hebrew vision of history was of God's being in total control without the nuance of human freedom. Also God's nature of self-giving love such as that revealed in Jesus Christ was glimpsed only dimly for a good part of Hebrew Scripture history.

At their best, however, the Hebrews were always able to conclude with the psalmist: "Yet you have brought us out to a spacious place" (66:12).

So I do not believe as some folks do that God is responsible for the trials and tribulations of our life, the tragic and troublesome things that happen to us. Some say that God sends these things to punish us or to chastise us. I don't believe that. I don't believe that God designs these tragic things and inflicts them upon us. Nor do I believe that the bad things that happen to us are punishment for our sin. I do believe, however, that God uses all these things to test us and shape us, to bring us to rich fulfillment. Everything that happens to us is not God's will, but there is a will of God in everything that happens.

I believe that what was happening in the story of Abraham's sacrifice of his son Isaac is a test. It was a test of Abraham's faith—whether he was going to trust God as the giver "of every good and perfect gift." You remember Isaac was a miracle child—a child given Abraham and Sarah when they were old. Abraham marveled in that gift; his son was life to him. We understand that better if we know a bit about the patriarchal system of Israel. Abraham was the patriarch. It was absolutely essential for a patriarch to have children so that the patriarchy could go on; therefore, having a son was really the future for Abraham.

So in this event Abraham is called to trust the Lord to provide the future. There is a marvelous promise in the Bible that says, "For surely I know the plans I have for you, says the Lord, plans for your welfare and not for harm, to give you a future with hope" (Jer. 29:11).

How we think and feel about God in relation to the tragic dimension of our life, our pain and suffering, shapes our whole life, certainly our praying. It helps us to always remember that life is not God. We do confuse the two. If we will remember that life isn't God, then we can affirm that though life isn't fair, God is good. God *uses* the circumstances of life to test and shape us. Prayer also becomes a testing, a testing of our relationship to God: to what degree do we trust God? How willing are we to put our lives in God's hands?

Also, in praying we *test* our longings, questions, needs, concerns, and desires. As we hold them up to God, especially when we pray with another or a group, we begin to see ourselves—our longings, needs, concerns, questions, and desires—in the perspective of our relationship to God and others. (See Day Seven.)

The whole process, then, is a part of the development of our trusting the Lord to provide the future.

DAY ONE

Personal Perspective through Praise

Matthew 6:13, KJV

For thine is the kingdom, and the power, and the glory, for ever. Amen.

Luke did not include this closing doxology in his record of the prayer Jesus taught his disciples. Scholars believe that very early in its life the church added this doxology as a kind of liturgical response to the original prayer. It was so much in keeping with the spirit of the prayer that Matthew made it an integral part. From the beginning, individuals and the church at worship have added this mighty outburst of praise, "For thine is the kingdom, and the power, and the glory, for ever. Amen."

We've been living with this model of Jesus, these directions that he gave us. Hopefully you will continue to live with it and find ways to make it a part of your daily experience.

During this phase of our adventure, we want to consider some basic ingredients of prayer and to discover for ourselves a pattern for praying.

Jesus and all those who would teach us to pray include *adoration* and *praise* as a basic ingredient of prayer.

Adoration: "Our Father who art in heaven, Hallowed be thy name" (RSV).
Praise: "For thine is the kingdom, and the power, and the glory, for ever. Amen" (KJV).

Adoration and praise make one movement in prayer. We adore God for who God is; we praise God for what God is doing.

Romans 11:33-36

O the depth of the riches and wisdom and knowledge of God! How unsearchable are his judgments and how inscrutable his ways! "For who has known the mind of the Lord? Or who has been his counselor? Or who has given a gift to him, to receive a gift in return?" For from him and through him and to him are all things. To him be glory forever. Amen.

There is always a dimension of mystery about prayer. Creature meets Creator. Praise and adoration enact the movement of "taking off our shoes" as we stand on holy ground. The Psalms are excellent resources for praise and adoration. Many people find it helpful to read a psalm or two each day as an act of praise and adoration at the beginning of the period of private prayer.

Others commit certain psalms or parts of psalms to memory and use these over and over again in adoring and praising God. Here are some favorites.

Psalm 100

Make a joyful noise to the LORD, all the earth.
Worship the LORD with gladness;
come into his presence with singing.

Know that the LORD is God.
It is he that made us, and we are his;
we are his people, and the sheep of his pasture.

Enter his gates with thanksgiving,
and his courts with praise.
Give thanks to him, bless his name.

For the LORD is good;
his steadfast love endures forever,
and his faithfulness to all generations.

Psalm 103:1-5

Bless the LORD, O my soul,
and all that is within me, bless his holy name.
Bless the LORD, O my soul,
and do not forget all his benefits—
who forgives all your iniquity,
who heals all your diseases,
who redeems your life from the Pit,
who crowns you with steadfast love and mercy,
who satisfies you with good as long as you live
so that your youth is renewed like the eagle's.

Psalm 8:1, 3-5, 9

O LORD, our Sovereign,
how majestic is your name in all the earth!

When I look at your heavens, the work of your fingers,
the moon and the stars that you have established;
what are human beings that you are mindful of them,
mortals that you care for them?

You have made them a little lower than God,
and crowned them with glory and honor.

O LORD, *our Sovereign,*
how majestic is your name in all the earth!

There is power in praise. Focusing on the greatness, love, mercy, care, presence, and power of God lifts us above our own limitations. It directs our minds to a source of strength beyond ourselves. We gain perspective for our own time and circumstances. I find, and many others have shared the same experience, that problems are seen in a different light, perplexities untangle, confusion often vanishes. A power unsought and unasked for comes when, in my praying, I can give attention to adoration and praise. I don't know how this works, but it does work.

Von Hugel once declared, "Any religion that ignores the adoration of God is like a triangle with one side left out."[7] There is an ancient Hindu prayer that says only, "Wonderful, wonderful, wonderful." When we think of God's activity in our lives, when we remember what God has done for us and for the world in Jesus Christ, we are moved to adoration and praise: "Wonderful, wonderful, wonderful."

Adoration and praise are mixtures of gratitude, reverence, and awe.

Gratitude: not only for God's gifts, but for God and God's revelation in Jesus Christ, for God's power that comes through the abiding presence of the Holy Spirit, for God's constancy—-always being there, always for us, always concerned.

Reverence: not a reverence that we ought to feel, but a firsthand feeling of being drawn into God's presence, drawn to the pinnacle of our own being, drawn to a feeling of oneness with others because of our oneness with God.

Awe: a feeling of being humble, unable to comprehend the mystery of God's love and grace moving in our lives. The speechless certainty that the coincidences that seem unexplainable have such meaning and purpose that we recognize them as "God-incidents," events in which the ever-present activity of God seems especially awe-invoking. The stirring within that makes us *know* that the sudden bursts of insight, the instant guidance, the falling into place of misplaced and displaced experiences are not accidental. All this Power beyond us breaking in and Mystery operating in our lives fill us with awe. "What are human beings that you are mindful of them, and mortals that you care for them?"

Gratitude, reverence, awe—like seeing a beautiful mountain rising out of the darkness at daybreak and not wanting to climb it or photograph it or talk about it, only to look at it and lose yourself in its grandeur; like walking with a friend, talking and sharing more and more deeply until you are one with each other, then sitting to rest and talking no more, only to be in each other's presence in silence; like sitting on the beach and hearing the torrential rush of the waves as a storm is rising: The waves get higher and higher and closer and closer, but you are not afraid, only overcome with the power of it all and your inability to calm them or hold them back.

Reflecting and Recording

Reread the psalms (100; 103:1-5; 8:1, 3-5, 9). Read them aloud, slowly and deliberately. Then read them a second time with all the exuberance and feeling they evoke. Then sit quietly for three minutes, five if you can, in *gratitude, reverence,* and *awe.*

■ ■ ■

After this time of adoration and praise, write two or three sentences that describe your feelings.

During the Day

Be sensitive to God-incidents today, bursts of insight, instant guidance, mystery, power breaking in. When you are aware of such, respond to it with this burst of praise, "Bless the LORD, O my soul, and all that is within me, bless his holy name." Get that in your mind now for your instant recall. Take a small piece of paper and a pen with you and note each time you become aware of God-incidents today.

DAY TWO

Confession for Communion and Cleansing

Yesterday you were asked to note your "God-incidents." Transfer these notes to this space now. If you didn't make notes, try to remember them and write them here.

Begin a brief prayer of adoration and praise with the words of the psalmist, "Bless the LORD, O my soul, and all that is within me, bless his holy name." Complete the prayer with your own words of adoration and praise as you think about who God is, what God has done and is doing, particularly how you may have seen God at work yesterday.

Confession is another basic ingredient in prayer. Through confession we experience cleansing and communion. The classic book *Cloud of Unknowing* uses the phrase *a lump of sin*. The writer says that we feel that way sometimes—like "a lump of sin." That came home to me vividly when I was traveling for two weeks away from my family many years ago. I came into New York from a transatlantic flight, tired, longing for my family, especially for my wife. A rather subtle but direct temptation presented itself. A young woman made herself available to me. I confess that my lust level almost got out of hand. I entertained the possibility of responding—only for a moment.

Out of commitment to my wife and family and all that I believe about life and relationship, I acted responsibly and refused the temptation. Yet that lustful moment stayed with me as a kind of blur almost the entire night.

My sleep schedule was in chaos because of the night flight from London and the change of time. Alone in my hotel, in my wakefulness, I wanted to pray, to be in close communion with God. I didn't seem capable of it, and communion didn't seem possible. After much mental wrestling and anguish, I became aware of the block. I was experiencing a "hangover" from the lustful moment I had experienced earlier. So I was feeling a tremendous sense of estrangement and emptiness. I felt like "a lump of sin."

That estrangement and emptiness was not due to something I'd done—I hadn't acted irresponsibly—but to the way I related to my lustful feelings. I confess that I didn't want to admit I had potentially lustful desires, but there they were—they were a real part of me with which I had to deal. Not wanting to find them, I felt like "a lump of sin."

Earlier in our adventure we worked on naming ourselves before God, sharing our honest selves with God. I practiced that by naming my "lump of sin," confessing it as a real part of me, asking God to help me use the vital energy behind it in more constructive ways. I began to experience relief and ease in my inner being. I began to feel "right" (honest) with God, and communication flowed. Soon I was relieved, uplifted, no longer feeling like "a lump of sin," and before too many minutes I was sleeping soundly. *Communion and cleansing had come through confession.* The psalmist knew the power of this long ago.

Psalm 66:16-20

Come and hear, all you who fear God,
and I will tell what he has done for me.
I cried aloud to him,
and he was extolled with my tongue.

If I had cherished iniquity in my heart,
*   the LORD would not have listened.*
But truly God has listened;
*   he has given heed to the words of my prayer.*

Blessed be God,
*   because he has not rejected my prayer*
*   or removed his steadfast love from me.*

Adoration and praise are there. And also confession: "If I had cherished iniquity in my heart, the LORD would not have listened."

The loving God to whom we pray wants fellowship with us. Because we know God is good and righteous, our sin prevents intimate communion. The block is on our side, not God's. The block is removed by confession. The writer of First John was not laying down a condition to be met, so much as stating a fact that is eternal, when he said, "If we confess our sins, he who is faithful and just will forgive us our sins and cleanse us from all unrighteousness" (1 John 1:9).

God's forgiveness is ours for the accepting. Confession is a prerequisite, not to God's forgiveness but to our appropriation (receiving) of God's forgiveness. That's the reason confession brings cleansing. We lay ourselves out before God. We accept God's love and forgiveness and are free and whole again.

Confession opens the door to communion. Sin brings separation, estrangement; forgiveness brings reconciliation, togetherness. Sin, then, is a barrier to communion. Confession removes the barrier. We come to God as we are, receive God's forgiveness, which makes us feel clean, and enter into communion with God.

Reflecting and Recording

Sin is not only what we do, it is often what we think and are. It is our separation from God, our failure to live in obedient relationship to God. It is putting our kingdom, rather than God's kingdom, first. Sometimes we feel like "a lump of sin," not because of what we have done but because our inner being seems out of joint, out of relationship with God. We don't feel any oneness. Our lives are fragmented, out of focus.

Where do you feel "out of joint" or estranged today? Write your confession here.

The fact that I am a sinner does not keep God from loving me. Communion with God does not depend upon my being without sin. On the contrary, it is dependent upon my acknowledging myself as a *sinner*, accepting that fact within myself, and believing with all my heart that God loves me just as I am, and that his love saves me, *cleanses* me.

When I believe in my heart in this way, I feel clean. I can enter into communion with God, praying something like this:

> God, I know that you are personal and that you are close by, but I have not acted accordingly. I am always forgetting that you are an infinitely loving Father and that your plan is to make me your child—fully, completely, with unimaginable benefits that only a loving father gives to his children. I keep forgetting that your uniqueness is not in being all-powerful but in being all-loving; that you are not only a God for me to love but also a God by whom I must allow myself to be loved. Help me, Father, to let myself be loved. Amen.

Finish the prayer that you started with your confession above by sharing with God exactly how you feel about accepting God's forgiveness and love.

During the Day

What we have been dealing with in this session of our adventure is perhaps the most difficult dimension of our relationship with God. We spend our lives struggling with God's love for us and what we are to do in response to that love. Here it is in a kind of scriptural nutshell.

1 John 4:7-12

Beloved, let us love one another, because love is from God; everyone who loves is born of God and knows God. Whoever does not love does not know God, for God is love. God's love was revealed among us in this way: God sent his only Son into the world so that we might live through him. In this is love, not that we loved God but that he loved us and sent his Son to be the atoning sacrifice for our sins. Beloved, since God loved us so much, we also ought to love one another. No one has ever seen God; if we love one another, God lives in us, and his love is perfected in us.

Select one person whom you have difficulty loving. During this day see how your deliberate effort to love this person as God has loved you enhances your communion with God.

DAY THREE

Power through Petition

Many persons who have lived a long life of prayer disparage petition as an unnecessary and almost irreverent attempt to get God to do what we want him to do. Prayer, they say, is primarily putting ourselves into the Father's hands, giving ourselves unreservedly to God, making no request other than for the doing of God's will. Prayer is an act of surrender, a willing openness to trust whatever the Father has for us.

Prayer is putting ourselves into the Father's hands, surrendering to God, opening ourselves to receive God's gifts. But to say that this leaves no place for petition (making our requests known to God) is to go against one of the most emphatic teachings of Jesus. The scriptures plainly state that we should come to the Father with our desires and ask God to meet our needs: Ask, knock, seek; "give us this day our daily bread"; "if two of you agree about anything you ask, it will be done for you"; "how much more will your Father give good things to those who ask."

We should not allow prayer to be reduced to the superstition that sees it as a desperate device for getting what we want (usually after all else has failed) or as merely a helpful psychological technique of autosuggestion. At the same time, we should not ignore the place of petition or supplication in an effective practice of prayer. Obviously, Jesus believed that there was power and meaning in petition and supplication. Paul put this ingredient of prayer into proper perspective in his letter to the Philippians.

Philippians 4:6-7

Do not worry about anything, but in everything by prayer and supplication with thanksgiving let your requests be made known to God. And the peace of God, which surpasses all understanding, will guard your hearts and your minds in Christ Jesus.

Different translations add different emphases.

NEB

Have no anxiety, but in everything make your requests known to God in prayer and petition with thanksgiving. Then the peace of God, which is beyond our utmost understanding, will keep guard over your hearts and your thoughts, in Christ Jesus.

PHILLIPS

Don't worry over anything whatever; whenever you pray tell God every detail of your needs in thankful prayer, and the peace of God, which surpasses human understanding, will keep constant guard over your hearts and minds as they rest in Christ Jesus.

Examine these different translations. Are there any substantial differences in meaning? What translation best opens up this passage for you? Why? Make some notes here.

Lewis Maclachlan in *The Teaching of Jesus on Prayer* makes this observation:

The expression of desires is no mean part of Christian worship. In contrast to other systems of prayer which teach the extinction of desire the New Testament encourages the development and discipline of our wants in accordance with the will of God. . . . Our desires are a very important factor in making us what we are, and if bad desires can be our ruin, good desires can be our salvation. Instead of trying to quench desire, we should purify and exalt it, and there is no better way of doing so than to make our requests known unto God. To state clearly what we want in the presence of God is an exercise which cannot be undertaken lightly or thoughtlessly. It is one important part of the discipline of prayer.[8]

After making the above statement Maclachlan warns us in this fashion:

1.   Beware of the weak desire of one who never wants anything enough to be sure of getting it, or of enjoying it when gotten.
2.   Beware, on the other hand, one very insistent and pressing desire whose satisfaction can retard the fulfillment of a higher purpose.
3.   Worst of all, and one of the chief hindrances to effectual prayer, is the divided desire. A double-minded person is unstable in all his or her ways. Putting those warnings in a positive fashion, we would say,
     a.   we must know what we want;
     b.   we must be sure that we want it;
     c.   we must not at the same time be asking for things that are contradictory to one another.

Reflecting and Recording

What were the last two or three specific petitions you made to God in prayer? Or what petitions are you bringing to God today? Write those here.

Test these petitions against the warnings sounded above. Do you know what you want? Are you sure that you want them? Are any of these requests in conflict with one another? Are they consistent with what you believe God wants and with the way God works in the world?

Having tested yourself, bring your petitions to God now. Pray specifically, verbalizing each request clearly, believing that what you ask "in his name" will be answered. Then ask God to help you identify that answer when it appears, however it appears.

During the Day

Yesterday we suggested that during the day you might note how your deliberate effort to love others as God has loved you enhances your communion with God. Hopefully you practiced that and found meaning in it. I want you to continue it today. Add this dimension to it: More often than not, God answers your prayers through others, and God answers others' prayers through you. As you express care in your relationships today, see your *loving* as an answer to the prayers of the person to whom you are showing love. In doing this you enter into a deliberate prayer partnership with God; *you practice living prayer.* See if this makes any difference in your relationships.

DAY FOUR

Power through Petition

There is no such thing as an unanswered prayer. Jesus taught us that if we pray with faith, then God will assuredly respond to our prayer. This stance of Jesus is psychologically sound. Think about it.

1. All desires tend to fulfill themselves if backed by expectation.
2. Our deepest desires and habitual thoughts create and control the conditions in which we live.
3. We are motivated and energized by our faith, by our desires, by the aims and goals of our lives.

There is something demonic as well as holy in the dynamic possibilities of our desires. It is true that we usually get that upon which we set our hearts. Therefore, we need to remember always that success is not in maximizing our self-interest but in living in interdependence as a part of God's family. Our petitions then focus not on our self-interest but on our deep need for community and the needs of all humankind.

Because of the inherent power of desire, some people say prayer is merely autosuggestion. The only thing wrong with that statement is the word *merely*. Prayer may be autosuggestion but not *merely* autosuggestion. And what is wrong with autosuggestion? Recall Paul's word to the Philippians.

Philippians 4:6-7

Do not worry about anything, but in everything by prayer and supplication with thanksgiving let your requests be made known to God. And the peace of God, which surpasses all understanding, will guard your hearts and your minds in Christ Jesus.

Paul continued that letter with these words from verse 8:

Finally, beloved, whatever is true, whatever is honorable, whatever is just, whatever is pure, whatever is pleasing, whatever is commendable, if there is any excellence and if there is anything worthy of praise, think about these things.

What we set our minds and hearts upon is likely to come to us. This makes the ingredient of petition in prayer even more important. In prayer, we not only increase our faith; we enlighten it. Our way of thinking may be changed and our desires purified as we bring them to God.

If we are truly praying, then our reason for bringing our petitions to God is to gain the assurance of God's will and to be directed in God's way. Petition functions in our praying to assist us in clarifying and stating our desires in terms of God's will. Whatever we do in prayer, whether adoring, praising, meditating, interceding, we are attempting to communicate with God and reach God's will. As we achieve God's will in prayer, we can be sure of achieving it in our lives.

The most active and persistent part of our nature is our desires and aspirations. Bringing these desires and aspirations to God in prayer and consecration is as much God-centered as adoration and meditation.

One of the common weaknesses of our prayer lives is the vagueness of our focus. We tend to read scripture or some devotional literature, praise God a little, get some good feelings, and be done with it. Petition saves us from that. It forces us to be specific, to be precise, to clarify our wants and desires, to seek to know our own minds in order to make them known to God.

Prayer might become more meaningful to us if our time of prayer became a time of knowing our own minds—clarifying and specifying our wants and desires, our hopes and dreams, our problems and perplexities, our sin and suffering. Then, in petition, we request the help of God's ever-present Spirit and power.

When I am this serious about petition, I find my petitions changing, certainly modified on presentation to God. "Prayer always changes our prayers." If we don't know what we ought to pray for (and often most of us don't know), we ask for God's guidance in our praying. This is the highest petition.

Reflecting and Recording

Adding the ingredient of petition to our praying necessarily requires that we expect answers. It is futile, even sacrilege, to ask God for something and not expect some response. Therefore, it's a good idea to keep a record of our requests and the answers God gives.

Go back to Day Seven of the first week of your adventure. Look at the *wishes* you were asked to list on that day. What has happened to those desires? Have they been fulfilled? List them here again with a word about what has happened.

Go back now to Day Five of the second week of your adventure. On that day you listed three bold requests to God. Note those again here with a word about what has happened to those requests.

How important were those petitions to you? You may not have gotten some of the things for which you asked. Is God saying no to you? Or are the requests still open to be fulfilled? Were you double-minded, making conflicting requests? Think now of the petitions you wish to bring to God. You may want to repeat some of the ones you've listed above or list some new ones. Test them by what we've been saying today and yesterday about petition. Write down the petitions you made yesterday that have not yet been answered. List them and add whatever you wish here.

During the Day

You may wish to share your most important petitions with a friend, someone with whom you have prayed before, maybe someone who is sharing this adventure with you. This is a good way to test your petitions. You can't be vague if you are going to share with another; you have to be clear in order to communicate. A trusted friend will be able to help you see it clearly, to be single-minded. Above all, a petition that is agreed upon by another will have the focus and power of Jesus' promise: "If two of you agree on earth about anything you ask, it will be done for you by my Father in heaven" (Matt. 18:19).

DAY FIVE

Intercession: "Turning the Question Mark into an Exclamation Point"

John 17:1-3, 9-11, 13-21, 24

After Jesus had spoken these words, he looked up to heaven and said, "Father, the hour has come; glorify your Son so that the Son may glorify you, since you have given him authority over all people, to give eternal life to all whom you have given him. And this is eternal life, that they may know you, the only true God, and Jesus Christ whom you have sent.

"I am asking on their behalf; I am not asking on behalf of the world, but on behalf of those whom you gave me, because they are yours. All mine are yours, and yours are mine; and I have been glorified in them. And now I am no longer

in the world, but they are in the world, and I am coming to you. Holy Father, protect them in your name that you have given me, so that they may be one, as we are one. . . . But now I am coming to you, and I speak these things in the world so that they may have my joy made complete in themselves. I have given them your word, and the world has hated them because they do not belong to the world, just as I do not belong to the world. I am not asking you to take them out of the world, but I ask you to protect them from the evil one. They do not belong to the world, just as I do not belong to the world. Sanctify them in the truth; your word is truth. As you have sent me into the world, so I have sent them into the world. And for their sakes I sanctify myself, so that they also may be sanctified in truth.

"I ask not only on behalf of these, but also on behalf of those who will believe in me through their word, that they may all be one. As you, Father, are in me and I am in you, may they also be in us, so that the world may believe that you have sent me. . . . Father, I desire that those also, whom you have given me, may be with me where I am, to see my glory, which you have given me because you loved me before the foundation of the world."

Jesus knew that the cross was imminent. Soon he would be "returning to the Father." He did that which was natural, that which reflected the style of his life and ministry: He turned his attention to others. Here is his love and hope translated into prayer for his disciples and for all who would be his disciples.

Father, keep the men you gave me by your power that they may be one . . . may my joy be completed in them . . . I am not praying that you will take them out of the world but that you will keep them from the evil one . . . make them holy . . . I consecrated myself for their sakes . . . I am not praying only for these men but for all those who will believe in me through their message . . . I want those whom you have given me to be with me where I am; I want them to see that glory which you have made mine. (AP)

Jesus prayed for others as simply and naturally as he prayed for himself. It should be no less true with us. There is a sense in which we are most like Jesus when we are expressing our love and concern for others in intercession on their behalf.

Stop here for a few minutes to think what it must have meant to the disciples two thousand years ago to have Jesus praying for them.

■ ■ ■

Think what it means that in praying for his disciples and those who would believe through their message, Jesus' prayer now includes you.

■ ■ ■

The living Christ is praying for you *now*: "Consequently he is able for all time to save those who approach God through him, since he always lives to make intercession for them" (Heb. 7:25). Ponder this: *Jesus' prayers then are affecting you now.* In addition, *Christ intercedes for you now.* What does this do for you? Immerse yourself in this truth for a few minutes.

■ ■ ■

There is no larger question mark in living prayer than there is about *intercession*. For many this is a great stumbling block to prayer. Despite all the questions and confused understandings, the fact remains: It is the natural mood of living prayer to pray for others as we pray for ourselves. When we are not "hung up" with intellectual problems, we move, almost inevitably, to lifting to God our concern for other persons.

It is not our task in this workbook to deal with the problems and questions surrounding *intercession*. Entire books have been written on the subject. Since this is an adventure, a workbook, the task at hand is to adventure into intercessory prayer. Such an adventure, I am convinced, will change our question mark into an exclamation point.

People who practice living prayer can heap witness upon witness to the power of intercession. It is an experiential fact that has been demonstrated over and over again, that if in any community a large number of earnest Christians unite in unselfish prayer for a revival of Christian concern and commitment, that revival will come. Dr. John R. Mott, world Christian leader of another generation, confirmed this in his testimony: "For many years it has been my practice in traveling among the nations to make a study of the sources of spiritual movements which are doing most to vitalize and transform individuals and communities. At times it has been difficult to discover the hidden spring, but invariably where I have had the time and patience to do so, I have found it in an intercessory prayer-life of great reality."[9]

Witness can be heaped upon witness of the "coincidences" that occur when we practice intercession. Archbishop William Temple said, "When I pray, coincidences happen, and when I do not, they don't."[10] Obviously these are not coincidences, but the realization of God-incidences.

Even though we "see through a glass darkly" and are often confused and baffled, our experience is clear that something creative and powerful happens when we practice intercessory prayer.

Harry Emerson Fosdick puts intercession in its clearest perspective:

No explanation, however reasonable, can do justice to the *experience* of vicarious praying. To feel that, we must turn to life. When a mother prays for her wayward son, no words can make clear the vivid reality of her supplications. Her love pours itself out in insistent demand that her boy must not be lost. She is sure of his value, with which no outward thing is worthy to be compared, and of his possibilities which no sin of his can ever make her doubt. She will not give him up. She follows him through his abandonment down to the gates of death; and if she loses him through death into mystery beyond, she still prays on in secret, with intercession which she may not dare to utter, that wherever in the moral universe he may be, God will reclaim him. As one considers such an experience of vicarious praying, [one] sees that it is not merely resignation to the will of God; it is urgent assertion of a great desire. She does not really think that she is persuading God to be good to her son, for the courage in her prayer is due to her certain faith that God also must wish that boy to be recovered from his sin. She rather is taking on her heart the same burden that God has . . . ; is joining her demand with the divine desire. In this system of personal life which makes up the moral universe, she is taking her place alongside God in an urgent, creative outpouring of sacrificial love.

Now, this mother does not know and cannot know just what she is accomplishing by her prayers. But we know that such mothers save their sons when all others fail. The mystery of prayer's projectile force is great, but the certainty of such prayer's influence, one way or another, in working redemption for needy lives is greater still. It may be, . . . that God has so ordained the laws of human interrelationship that we can help one another not alone by our deeds but also directly by our thoughts, and that earnest prayer may be the exercise of this power in its highest terms. But whether that mother has ever argued out the theory or not, she still prays on. Her intercession is the utterance of her life; it is love on its knees.[11]

Reflecting and Recording

Examine your experience of praying for others. Has it been a *big* part of your life? How much time have you invested in it? Do you believe any difference is made by your praying for others? What difference? Make some notes as you reflect upon your experience of intercessory prayer.

What experience have you had that confirms the power of other people praying for you?

Read again Fosdick's word about intercession.

■ ■ ■

During the Day

Go through this day conscious of the fact that Christ's prayers in the past affect you now, and that he continually intercedes for you. Believing that his prayers are powerful in your life, pray for others with whom you come in contact, believing that your prayers are powerful in their lives.

DAY SIX

Intercession: A Ministry of Love

It is the testimony of people who practice living prayer that things happen when we pray that do not happen when we don't pray. People are healed, situations change, conditions are altered, persons find direction, revivals come, even the courses of nations are redirected.

It appears that God has so ordered life and the world that our praying is a vital part of the redemptive plan for individuals and the entire universe. Through intercessory prayer God does something that would not otherwise be done. There are numerous facets to intercessory prayer, some that we have experienced, no doubt many that are yet undiscovered. There is one dimension that is such a part of life that we need to give it attention now in our adventure in living prayer. Intercessory prayer is a ministry of love and care.

Consider the possibilities for such a ministry.

1. Intercession is an identification of love. Clarence Jordan, in his *Cotton Patch Gospel* version of the New Testament, translates that signal word in 2 Cor. 5:19: "In Christ God was reconciling the world to himself . . ." in this fashion: "God was in Christ, hugging the world to Himself."

That's what we do when we pray. We put our arms around another person, a relationship, a situation, our community—even the world—and hug it to ourselves and to God in love. In a mysterious way that we may never understand, something always happens to us, and sometimes in those for whom we pray.

2. Intercessory prayer opens our minds to hear what else God wants to tell us about the way we can minister to others. When we pray for another person, we are centered on that person as well as on God. God can then speak to us about the needs of that other person and how we may be instruments of meeting that need.

3. Intercessory prayer becomes the "launching pad" for our service to others. People often say, "Prayer *alone* is not enough." Frank Laubach, the great practitioner of intercession, reminds us that "prayer that seeks to do God's will is not alone. It will be accompanied by any other approach that God may suggest. It will be accompanied by service, by considerations, by kindnesses of every kind."[12]

4. Intercessory prayer becomes the "power base" for our relationships with others. In my ministry I find that when I pray for persons with whom I am counseling

immediately before I see them, the counseling experience is far more effective than when I don't. There was a period in my life when I did not take intercessory prayer seriously. During that time I always felt somewhat frantic and hassled—almost always under pressure for the next appointment or too intense in my relationship with the person with whom I was sharing. Then I began to practice intercessory prayer, always reserving time between appointments to pray for the person with whom I would be counseling. It was revolutionary for me. I was more relaxed in my relationships, sharper in my perception, focused in my attention—but more, something happened in the persons for whom I prayed. They were more relaxed, more open and honest in their sharing, more receptive to me and what I had to offer, willing to accept my inability and often unwillingness to give advice.

Intercessory prayer was the "power base" for my relationships with them. This can be transferred into every area of life. We are empowered to serve others, and we serve with the greatest insight and effectiveness when we pray for those we seek to serve.

5. Intercessory prayer is the investment of ourselves in God's design for God's kingdom among people and nations. Frank Laubach called for a "prayer army" of ten million people who "would start praying until our minds were in perfect harmony with the will of God . . . who would tip the balance and save the world." He called this a "war of amazing kindness." We have yet to see what could happen should such an army arise!

Praying for people will bring you to love them. Loving them will lead you to serve them. Serving them will be the open door through which God can move in to save, heal, and make whole.

The ministry of intercession is very demanding. To be serious about intercession is to be ready to give ourselves for the sake of others. This may be the reason we don't take intercession to heart. Here it is at its deepest level.

Exodus 32:30-32

On the next day Moses said to the people, "You have sinned a great sin. But now I will go up to the LORD; perhaps I can make atonement for your sin." So Moses returned to the LORD and said, "Alas, this people has sinned a great sin; they have made for themselves gods of gold. But now, if you will only forgive their sin—but if not, blot me out of the book that you have written."

That's about as far as one can go in prayer, isn't it? . . . a willingness to be "blotted out" for others.

We hear Jesus saying such things as:

Luke 22:28-32

You are those who have stood by me in my trials; and I confer on you, just as my Father has conferred on me, a kingdom, so that you may eat and drink at my table in my kingdom, and you will sit on thrones judging the twelve tribes of Israel. Simon, Simon, listen! Satan has demanded to sift all of you like wheat, but I have prayed for you that your own faith may not fail; and you, when once you have turned back, strengthen your brothers.

Imagine the depth and intensive prayer commitments Jesus had for Peter (Simon). Jesus wept over the city:

Luke 13:34

Jerusalem, Jerusalem. . . . How often have I desired to gather your children together as a hen gathers her brood under her wings, and you were not willing!

Is there any cause to which we are so committed that it evokes this kind of anguish? Intercessory prayer is not easy. It demands the investment not only of our prayer energy but of our total lives. When we pray sincerely and earnestly for others, we become unselfish. The blessing of the other person or situation for which we are praying becomes our dominant desire. This clears a channel through which we move in service or through which God moves directly. We put our whole selves into other persons and great causes. We ally ourselves with God for the sake of the persons we care about and the purposes we serve.

Our commitment to intercessory prayer is probably not waiting for some explanation of how it works but for a love and passion great enough to drive us to it.

Reflecting and Recording

Recall the one occasion (person, situation, experience) in which you invested the most energy in intercessory prayer. List it here.

1. What was the outcome of that situation? What changes took place in the person or situation for which you were praying? What changes took place in you? Record your answers here.

2. Have you ever prayed for someone or some situation and were led to do something *yourself* in response? Name one or two situations and what you were led to do.

3. Is there a person or are there persons or situations about whom or about which you are *deeply* concerned today? Name two or three.

Are you concerned enough to pray for these persons or situations daily? If so, this is your prayer list. You may want to put these names or situations on a card or small piece of paper in order to carry them with you so that you can take them out a number of times during the day to pray for them. Make a commitment to at least remember them in prayer each day for the balance of this adventure in living prayer.

During the Day

If you made a list of your prayer concerns, take it with you. See how many times today you have the opportunity to pray for the persons or situations you listed under question 3.

DAY SEVEN

Follow a Pattern until You Need No Pattern

On Day One of this phase of our adventure we talked about the place of adoration and praise in our praying. Perhaps you have memorized one of the sample psalms that was printed there, or some other favorite. If so, repeat it slowly as you begin this period today. If you haven't, read this one slowly, letting the words seep into your whole being.

Psalm 46:1-5, 10-11

God is our refuge and strength,
  a very present help in trouble.
Therefore, we will not fear, though
    the earth should change,
  though the mountains shake in the heart of the sea;
though its waters roar and foam,
  though the mountains tremble with its tumult.
There is a river whose streams make glad the city of God,
  the holy habitation of the Most High.
God is in the midst of the city; it shall not be moved;
  God will help it when the morning dawns. . . .
"Be still, and know that I am God!
  I am exalted among the nations,
  I am exalted in the earth."
The LORD of hosts is with us;
  the God of Jacob is our refuge.

Now, be as still and quiet as you can. Free your mind of any thoughts of what you have to do later today. Become as conscious of God as possible. Believe that God is as near as the air you breathe. Maybe you need to think about some images of God, making affirmations like this:

1. God is light, and in God there is no darkness at all!
2. God is love—and God so loved the world that he gave his Son!
3. God is not far from any one of us, because in God we live and move and have our being.

When you have become as conscious of God as you possibly can, bring into your consciousness of God the names of the persons or situations you listed yesterday as deep concerns of prayer. Do only this. Bring each person or situation, one by one, into your consciousness of God. Spend five minutes doing this. To cultivate a consciousness of God you may want to start all over with Psalm 46:1-5, 10-11, followed by the affirmations concerning God. Then bring persons and situations into that consciousness. Spend five minutes doing this.

■ ■ ■

The exercise you have just completed is often the way I practice intercessory prayer. Many times we begin to pray for people or situations—asking God to bless, change, intervene, or do something we think God ought to do—without becoming aware of God's presence in our lives. Two important ingredients of intercessory prayer are in the preceding exercise: (a) God-consciousness for ourselves; (b) centered or focused thinking and praying on behalf of other persons or situations. These ingredients are necessary for power to become effective in our lives and through us to others. They are also necessary for us to become clear receivers of whatever message God wants to give us about the subject of our praying.

Now to our main concern today: In developing a life of living prayer, most of us need to follow a pattern of prayer until no pattern is necessary. Many prayer periods are ineffective because we are unable to stay with them, to center down, or focus. There is no direction in which we are going. Prayer needs direction. This is that creative discipline we are seeking to cultivate within our natural but sporadic inclinations to pray.

Each person must find his or her own pattern, and that's what practice will do for us. Here are two common patterns—one for morning and one for evening—with which you may experiment until you find a more effective style.

Morning

It is vitally important that early in the day we seek God's strength and guidance. Even the busiest persons can find time for this.

Upon waking, turn your thoughts at once to God. Repeat beneath your breath, or even aloud, "This is the day the LORD has made: I will rejoice and be glad in it." Or "Bless the LORD, O my soul; and all that is within me, bless his holy name!" Or repeat a verse of a hymn or poem that is especially meaningful to you. Then when you can settle in your private room to which Jesus told us to go, this scheme suggested by W. E. Sangster, which has been helpful to thousands, may be helpful to you.

Adoration: Think about the greatness of God, the incredibility that God is listening to you and is going to answer. Offer praise to God for who God is. "Hallowed be thy name!"

Thanksgiving: "Count your many blessings, name them one by one—then it will surprise you what the Lord has done." Health, home, love, work, friends, fun, family. Even those who are suffering ill health or misfortune can find something for which to express gratitude to God.

Dedication: Even though you have dedicated yourself to God in a whole-life fashion, every day ought to be the occasion to renew that dedication to God.

Guidance: Seek God's guidance for the day. Try to foresee what the day is going to be like, what you are going to be doing, people you will be meeting. Think how things are going to be—each thing, each person—because God is with you. Try to get in touch with that to which God is calling you, not just with how he has used you in the past.

Intercession: Pray for others. A prayer list will help to keep you faithful in this. This is so important that we dare not be casual about it.

Petition: We have considered the place of petition in prayer. Jesus has given us promises that we should accept and upon which we should act. Make your petitions to God in the spirit of wanting to do God's will and find God's way in your life.

Meditation: It's a good thing to spend a few minutes at the close of your prayer period thinking about or brooding over some truth or insight or experience, giving your mind to God that you may think God's thoughts after him.

Evening

As it is important to begin the day with God, likewise it is to end it. Many people say their prayers at night, but there is not too much focus and usually a lot of petition or general "bless _____ and _____ and _____." Evening prayer can be as focused as morning. The following pattern may be helpful to you.

Adoration: Again focus on God by offering words of praise.

Confession: Review the day, look at your life, make your confession of failure, pretense, exaggeration, lack of love, dishonesty, callousness, or shallowness in relationship. Don't just ask God to forgive your sins. Be specific as you look at life as you have lived it during one day. Accept God's forgiveness. If there is a chance for restitution, some action necessary for you to be reconciled to someone, make a plan to get at the reconciliation or restitution at the earliest possible time.

Thanksgiving: As you review the day you will find numerous things for which to be grateful. If you are attentive and sensitive to the workings of God, you will be able on many evenings to thank God for answering the prayer you prayed that morning.

Supplication: This is a kind of old-fashioned word that may have little meaning to you. It is like *intercession*. It is intercession and petition combined—a kind of brooding, longing act of remembrance of persons and situations about whom and which you are concerned. Bringing these in love and concern is an offering of them and your self to God.

(This pattern of evening prayer is easy to remember because the first letters of each movement spell ACTS. The ACTS of evening prayer are Adoration, Confession, Thanksgiving, Supplication.)

Perhaps you will need to adapt these patterns to your own schedule. If, for instance, you spend more time at prayer in the morning, you may wish to include the important dimension of confession at that time, reviewing your actions and responses to others during the preceding day.

Again, remember that no scheme is worth anything unless it helps in making prayer a living experience. Prayer is *alive* when we are experiencing communion with God. Devise a plan that works for you.

Reflecting and Recording

If you are doing this exercise in the morning, move through the scheme suggested for morning prayer. Go through each movement in your own way.

If it is evening, go through the movements of evening prayer in your own way.

In this space, record briefly your honest feelings about going through such a guided plan of prayer.

During the Day

If you haven't made a prayer list yet, maybe you are ready to do so. Jot down names and situations you want to carry with you in your prayer concern today. Recall them as often as possible.

Group Meeting
for Week Four

Introduction

One big failure in much of our praying is the failure to be aware of and sensitive to what is happening as a result of our praying. This failure happens at two levels. One, there are obvious answers to prayer that go unnoticed. Two, we are so intent upon finding the dramatic answers that we miss the subtle, deep changes of heart and mind taking place within us.

Living in friendship and fellowship with God, cooperating with God's Spirit, living a Christlike life in the world—which is the goal of prayer—requires conscious effort on our part. A primary focus of this effort is the development of our sensitivity. The basic ingredients of prayer you have been considering this week sharpen sensitivity.

Sharing with others is also helpful in the development of sensitivity. We need groups such as this to facilitate our sharing, but we also need to be intentional about sharing with persons who are not part of our group. Many persons are inspired to pray by the witness of persons who are finding meaning in prayer. Our prayer experience is deepened and expanded as we think seriously enough about it to search out what meaning it actually has for us—and to share that meaning with others.

Sharing Together

1. As you begin this session, select a person to read a couple of the selections from the Psalms recorded for Day One of this week; then sing one or two verses of a hymn everyone knows.

2. Let each person in the group tell the basic ingredients of prayer with which he or she has the most difficulty, and why.

3. On Day Four of this week you were asked to reflect upon what had happened to some needs, wishes, and requests you had recorded during the first and second weeks of the adventure. Share some meaningful results of that reflection. Was a prayer answered? How? Did you change your mind about a need or a request? Have there been "results" that you failed to note?

4. Many have had meaningful experiences of being prayed for. If you've had such an experience, share it with the group.

5. On Day Six the possibilities of intercessory prayer as a ministry of love were considered. What new insights about intercessory prayer came to you? What commitment did you make that you would like to share with the group?

6. Discuss the possibility of a group prayer list for which you will make intercession (as individuals and as a group) during the remainder of this adventure. If you decide to make this list, share your concerns and select no more than three or four of them on your list. (It is important that you consider concerns outside as well as within the group.) There is a limit to our capacity of prayer energy. Each week review your list to delete and add according to need and concern.

Praying Together

Most of us know the power of touch. A football player slaps the hand of a teammate. A friend places an arm around our shoulder as we stand at the grave of a loved one. A child throws arms around us for a joyous welcome home. Our husband or wife quietly takes our hand and holds it warmly or touches it only fleetingly at a moment in a group when we need reassurance. A handshake or a hug in parting is remembered long after words are forgotten.

Jesus took children on his knees to bless them. He often touched people to heal them. In prayer, also, the human touch is often important. We should not hesitate to hold a person's hand as we pray for him or her. It is a mystery, but somehow power—even the power of God—is transmitted person to person by touch.

Be sensitive in your group and in your personal relationships to the possible inherent power of the human touch. There may be occasions in your group, for instance, when you ask persons to allow you to place hands upon them as you pray for them. Miracles have come through groups gathering around a person and laying loving hands upon and praying for him or her.

1. If you have made a group prayer list, begin this time of praying together by centering in as a group in prayer for these persons and needs. You may wish to use the exercise suggested in today's section in the workbook as a way of centering in on these needs.

2. Earlier in your meeting persons were asked to share the ingredient of prayer with which they were having the most difficulty. Also, some may have shared a commitment to a ministry of intercessory prayer. Considering the needs expressed, have a time of special prayer now. Close your meeting by standing with your arms around each other in a circle.

   a. In two or three minutes of silence look into the eyes of the persons in your group and reflect upon what is happening in your life and in the lives of others.

   b. After this time of silence, let each person voice spontaneously what he or she is feeling now in a single word (for example, joy, frustration, hope, need).

   c. Close by singing the first verse of "Blest Be the Tie That Binds" or "They'll Know We Are Christians by Our Love."

Week Five

Pray without Ceasing

✠

INTRODUCTION
WEEK FIVE

The God to Whom We Pray

When I am asked to do a seminar or any kind of teaching event related to prayer, it doesn't matter how much time I have—whether a lot or a little—I always make sure that I talk a bit about the God to whom we pray. I believe it is absolutely essential to begin at this point because I believe prayer begins with God. Prayer is not my idea; it is God's idea.

When we know that, we can slough off all the strain and stress of trying to get God's attention, hoping that God will listen, struggling to speak the right words in order that God might accept what we say.

All of creation, especially the creation of humankind, is an expression of God's love and grace. Dionysus (the pseudo-Areopagite), a fourth century mystical theologian, argued that God created us because God yearned to love us.

Most of us know Augustine's famous words, "For thee were we made, O God, and our hearts are restless until they find their rest in thee."

Think about this. Could it be true from the other side—that God is restless, yearning, longing to be in relationship with us? Because of God's primary nature of love, God created us as free persons so that we could either receive or resist God's grace. Yet at the heart of everything is God's movement toward us.

You find it in scripture. The Christian story, recorded in both the Hebrew Scriptures and the New Testament, is not the story of human beings seeking God—it is the story of God seeking us.

So prayer is God's idea. Prayer begins with God. That means we always need to keep in mind the God to whom we pray. I want to offer three affirmations—simple ones but all profoundly relevant to prayer.

First, God cares about what happens to you. I believe that with all my heart, and I hope you will work on believing it. I know that not all the signs would indicate that. Sometimes our lives fall to pieces, and we are not sure at all that there is a God, much less that God cares for us. We need to remember that God is not responsible for what happens to us. There is sin and evil and human freedom—all of which are intimately linked—that bring about much of the chaos, confusion, and contradictions, as well as pain and suffering in our lives. As suggested earlier, we need to remember that life is not God—and though life is not fair, God is good.

Second, God hears you when you pray. Is anything more important than to be listened to?

As Christians, when we look for our clearest picture of God, we look to Jesus. One of the most characteristic dimensions of Jesus' life and ministry was the attention he gave to people around him. He heard blind Bartimaeus call out from the roadside. Jesus felt the touch of the woman who had been hemorrhaging for fourteen years when she reached out in the crowd and touched the hem of his garment. He saw Zacchaeus up in the sycamore tree. He listened to the leper who came to him and said, "If you want to, you can make me clean." Some of the tenderest words in scripture come in Jesus' response to that leper: "Of course I want to" (Matt. 8:2, PHILLIPS). If God is like Jesus, then we know that God hears us when we pray.

And then there is this third affirmation: God answers. Just as surely as we speak to God, as we seek God and seek to be related to God, just that surely God responds—God answers.

There is a marvelous word of the Lord, recorded by the prophet Isaiah, that speaks to this issue: "Before they call I will answer, while they are yet speaking I will hear" (Isa. 65:24). What an extravagant word—God hears and God answers. Even before the woman who had the issue of blood said anything, as she reached out in faith and touched the hem of Jesus' garment, he responded. Even before she spoke, Jesus heard.

Remembering these three affirmations will not only call us to prayer, it will shape our praying.

DAY ONE

"Day by Day, by Day, by Day"

In every age, we put our deepest experiences to music. Music is an important part of our worship. When we can't communicate the depth and breadth of our feelings, we set them to music. Hymns are rich resources for living prayer.

Millions of people have learned an old prayer through a new song. The hit tune in *Godspell*, "Day by Day," repeats the words of a prayer by Saint Richard of Chichester, who died in 1255. He prayed:

> Thanks be to thee, my Lord Jesus Christ, for all the benefits and blessings, which thou hast given to me, for all the pains and insults which thou hast borne for me. O most merciful Friend, Brother and Redeemer; may I know thee more clearly, love thee more dearly, and follow thee more nearly.

So today we sing it to popular music:

> Day by day, O dear Lord, three things I pray:
> to see thee more clearly,
> love thee more dearly,
> follow thee more nearly,
> day by day, by day, by day.

If you know the tune to this song, stop now and sing it aloud—at least hum it as you think about the meaning of the words. If you don't know the tune, make the prayer your own by praying it aloud.

■ ■ ■

Now stop and get the words in their modern rendering firmly in your mind. Paul wrote some advice to the Thessalonians that is good for us today.

1 Thessalonians 5:13-18

> *Be at peace among yourselves. And we urge you, beloved, to admonish the idlers, encourage the faint hearted, help the weak, be patient with all of them. See that none of you repays evil for evil, but always seek to do good to one another and to all. Rejoice always, pray without ceasing, give thanks in all circumstances; for this is the will of God in Christ Jesus for you.*

"Rejoice always, pray without ceasing, give thanks in all circumstances. . . ." Quite an order . . . but what a difference it makes in our lives, even to try it.

Obviously, this does not mean that we are to spend our lives in prayer meetings. It does mean that prayer becomes living prayer when we *pray* our lives, rather than *say* our prayers. Our goal is a life of prayer.

And we don't stumble into such a life of prayer. It comes from the deep desire to see God more clearly, to love God more dearly, and follow God more nearly. That is the purpose of this adventure.

We have deliberately refused to give one definition of prayer, for prayer cannot be defined in a few neat sentences. We heap words upon words seeking to define this movement of the individual to God, and God to the individual, but something is still missing. At the heart of prayer is communion—the "raising of the mind and heart to God." Whatever techniques or methods or plans we use, the *dynamic* is communion with God. The goal of prayer is a life of friendship and fellowship with God, *cooperation* with God's Spirit, living God's life in the world. That's what I mean by *living* prayer.

We must be intentional about seeking consciously to relate all of life to God. How do we get at that? We have already begun. The "During the Day" suggestions have been aimed at this. Now we want to spend an entire week deliberately focusing on the admonition of Paul to pray without ceasing.

I believe that we can consciously relate all of life to God only as we spend some deliberate and focused time with God in a specific period of prayer. For most people, I think this time should be at the *beginning* of the day. Our minds are fresh, work is ahead, the day is new. Life has been passive as we have slept; now life is active—we need to huddle deliberately with God in order to play the game with God in an effective way. I believe that most of us will always need that specific fifteen- to thirty-minute period at some time, when we take Jesus' advice and go into "our secret room" to be alone with God. You have been practicing that for the past four weeks, and I am sure it has made a difference in your life.

Reflecting and Recording

Turn back to the guides for prayer that were given yesterday. Take the guide that fits your situation now—morning, evening, or your own combination of the two—and pray by that guide. Simply, briefly, in your own words, without trying to be formal, pray by one of those guides. Take your time doing this.

Now in this space, try to write out briefly the prayer you have just prayed.

During the Day

Can you repeat the prayer "Day by Day" without referring to the words? If you can't, go back and review it. These words are printed on page 179 for you to take with you into the day. Whenever you are moved to think about it, pray it. You may want to sing it, hum it, or repeat it beneath your breath.

DAY TWO

Let Interruptions Call You to Prayer

We must be intentional about seeking consciously to relate all of life to God. This requires discipline. Here is a beginning. Pick out some regular interruptions in your daily life: stopping for a red traffic light, waiting for an appointment, standing in line at the grocery check-out stand, waiting for the commuter train or bus, filling your car with gas—a regular interruption that is a part of your life.

Decide now that during these interruptions you are going to pray the "Day by Day" prayer. Get it solidly in your mind now, because you will want to be able to call it to consciousness spontaneously.

Day by day, O dear Lord, three things I pray:
to see thee more clearly,
love thee more dearly,
follow thee more nearly,
day by day, by day, by day.

What you really want to fix firmly in your memory are those three petitions: to see thee more clearly, love thee more dearly, follow thee more nearly.

According to how much time your interruption gives you, you can approach your prayer time in all sorts of ways. Make the three petitions:

O Lord, I want to see thee more clearly, love thee more dearly, and follow thee more nearly.

Or you may want to take them one at a time—in the sequence of your interruptions. Meditate on what it means to see the Lord more clearly. Then at the next interruption, turn your mind to the desire to love Christ more dearly. And next, what would it mean in your life to follow him more nearly? Use the interruptions to pray this prayer so that as you return your attention to your situation, you will be more in touch with God's possibilities therein for your life—your relationship with the service station attendant, the check-out person, even the environment surrounding you as you drive along.

Leave this line of thinking for now, and give your attention to a dimension of prayer taught by Jesus.

Luke 18:1-8

Then Jesus told them a parable about their need to pray always and not to lose heart. He said, "In a certain city there was a judge who neither feared God nor had respect for people. In that city there was a widow who kept coming to him and saying, 'Grant me justice against my opponent.' For a while he refused; but later he said to himself, 'Though I have no fear of God and no respect for anyone, yet because this widow keeps bothering me, I will grant her justice, so that she may not wear me out by continually coming.'" And the Lord said, "Listen to what the unjust judge says. And will not God grant justice to his chosen ones who cry to him day and night? Will he delay long in helping them? I tell you, he will quickly grant justice to them. And yet, when the Son of Man comes, will he find faith on earth?"

Luke 11:11-13

"Is there anyone among you who, if your child asks for a fish, will give a snake instead of a fish? Or if the child asks for an egg, will give a scorpion? If you then, who are evil, know how to give good gifts to your children, how much more will the heavenly Father give the Holy Spirit to those who ask him!"

Reflecting and Recording

Go back and reread the scripture. When you have done so, write anything that comes to your mind in response. Let this be random thinking and writing. Don't try to organize it or to be systematic. Just write whatever comes to your mind in response to this scripture: words, questions, sentences—anything.

Close your period today by returning to the guide for morning and evening prayer. Use the one that fits your time frame now, and pray what you wish, following the guide. Spend as much time as is necessary with this.

During the Day

What regular "interruptions" will you experience today—waiting for an appointment or for the bus or in a grocery line or at the gas station? Think about the day ahead. List those "interruptions" here.

Determine now to use these interruptions consciously to relate your life to God—and through God, back to your present situation—by using the "Day by Day" prayer. You may want to review the way you can use the interruption and the prayer itself.

DAY THREE

Let Situations Call You to Prayer

Go back and read Luke 18:1-8, printed in your workbook for yesterday.

■ ■ ■

Now ask yourself:

1. What are the bare essentials of what is said there? All reading is an interpretation of what is written, but try to find what the scripture itself wants to say; try to hear just what is said and not what you would have it say. Record that here.

2. What does the scripture mean for you? What is Jesus trying to say to you in this passage? Here you will try to give your own interpretation to discover the significance of these words for your present situation. Write that meaning here.

3. If you decided to act upon the message of this scripture, what would that mean? Would there be any changes in your life? What changes? If you took this word of Jesus as a direct word to you, what would you have to do about it? Write your response here.

Now compare what you have written about the scripture today and what you wrote in your random response to it yesterday. These are two ways to read the scripture profitably. Both ways can have real meaning to your life.

Throughout this adventure, scripture has been a vital part of our daily experience. This has been deliberate. It is my contention that to have a vital life of prayer, it is essential to live with the scripture. This is one of the primary ways of discovering God, of communing with God, and of finding God's will. In the New Testament scripture Christ comes alive to us, and we come to know God through Christ. We will pursue this more next week, but let's begin the process now by considering this scripture, which has to do with our emphasis this week.

This parable of Jesus, "the unjust judge," has a twin parable—"the parable of the friend at midnight" (Luke 11:5-13). Both teach what is called *importunity* or *perseverance* in prayer. This perseverance may even mean remaining faithful and continuing to trust until the end of time. "When the Son of Man comes, will he find faith on earth?" (Luke 18:8). God is not like the reluctant friend or the unjust judge. God is like a loving parent. The main point of the parables is that there are times in our prayer life when we simply have to keep on praying. The man at midnight was prepared to keep on asking until the friend got out of bed and granted his request. The widow was willing to keep on pleading with the unjust judge until she was vindicated. God is neither like the friend at midnight nor the unjust judge, for God does not reluctantly withhold the gifts. Still, God cannot give all gifts at all times. Our persistence in prayer is not to nag God about our unsettled requests but to ingrain in us our ultimate trust and reliance on God for our future and what is to come.

We are going to come back to this later. For now, see this dimension of prayer as part of building a life of prayer, of praying without ceasing.

Shift gears now. Here is the truth we are trying to drive home: We must be intentional about seeking consciously to relate all of life to God. Here is another aid in this effort: Let situations call you to prayer.

A hurried shopper jostled a little girl who had just gotten a double dip of ice cream, and the delicious treat splashed on the floor. My heart went out to the little girl. The busy shopper was gone—didn't even see what had happened. The girl was completely surprised, shocked into a kind of numbness. From the look on her face, I could tell she had spent all her money with nothing to enjoy from it. I surmised that her mother was in another store of the shopping center.

I prayed. Like a flash, it all happened. I called the incident to the attention of the clerk who was busily helping others with their ice cream, laid the money for another cone on the counter, and asked her to offer the little girl a replacement for her lost treat. It was a thrill to see the little girl come out of shock and move from sadness to joy.

Elementary? Yes; but prayer for me is consciously seeking to relate all of life to God. Love was there; and where love is, God is.

Close this period by returning to the guide for morning and evening prayer given on Day Seven of the preceding week. Use whatever pattern you have devised that fits your time frame now, and pray what you wish, following your guide. Spend as much time as is necessary with this.

During the Day

Continue to pray the "Day by Day" prayer at your interruptions. Today let situations call you to prayer. You get the point of the incident that I gave. All sorts of situations develop in your life. Try consciously to relate God to these situations in prayer and action. To be deliberate about this, recall the model we considered earlier.

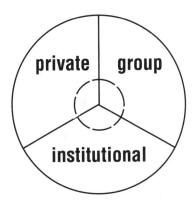

Situations in each of these arenas of our lives demand our prayer attention. List some of these situations in each area you anticipate today, in order to be deliberate in allowing situations to call you to prayer.

DAY FOUR

Let Persons Call You to Prayer

For three days now you have been experimenting with the "Day by Day" prayer. You are being intentional about seeking consciously to relate all of life to God. How is that effort working? What kinds of experiences are jostling your memory to recall this prayer? In your mind now, walk through the past three days. What interruptions are calling you to prayer? List them below.

Interruptions that are calling me to prayer are these:

What situations have called you to prayer? List these and write a brief word about each situation and how you prayed. You may want to try to recall your actual prayer and write it here.

Another signal that will assist us in praying without ceasing is this: Let persons call you to prayer.

It is amazing how experiences that ordinarily would appear mundane take on extraordinary import when we are intentionally seeking to relate all of life to God.

On September 26, 1993, I was flying from Memphis to Lubbock, Texas. Since I had to be in Lubbock to preach at 7:00 on Sunday evening, I had to catch a plane out of Memphis at 1:00 P.M. That meant I had to leave immediately after our worship service at noon. It was rush, rush, rush, all the way. When I got to the airport, I learned that my flight had been delayed for an hour, which meant that I would not make my connection in Dallas. It was a trying, frustrating, hectic experience. The ticket agents were gracious and generous and sought to do everything they could to facilitate my getting to Lubbock in time to preach that evening. When I finally made it to Dallas where I was to change planes for Lubbock, I was frustrated and frazzled. My nerves were beginning to jangle. I had to run with my bags a long distance, and I even had some pain in my chest. The thought struck me—do you suppose it is a heart attack? As I settled in my seat on the flight from Dallas to Lubbock, grateful that I was going to get there on time, I began to pray. It was the attendant who called me to prayer. She was so kind and gracious as I boarded the plane, and her greeting cheered me up. As I settled in to pray, I prayed for her. As we were landing in Lubbock, the same attendant who had greeted me with such uplifting cheer came on the intercom to instruct us about landing and give us words about the airport in Lubbock. She finished her instruction by saying, "I hope you have a good stay in Lubbock, and may God bless you."

I have traveled all over the world and I travel all the time, but that was the first time in my experience that an airline attendant had used those words, "God bless you." It provided the finishing encouragement and uplift for me to begin my preaching mission in Lubbock in a good way.

Persons call us to deep and meaningful prayer. Other than those persons to whom we relate daily and for whom we pray constantly, there are those persons we meet in brief, one-time encounters who need our affirmation, even petition and intercession. I believe that the climate of relationships—even the relationship of casual contacts with strangers—can be changed by prayer. This is precisely how using our interruptions for prayer can put us into much stronger relationships with those around us. When we consciously seek to relate a person whom we meet to God, a power is released about which we know little but which can make a significant difference in that person's life. Aside from that, it will also make a tremendous difference in our lives.

There's a verse of scripture in the Book of Job that describes how crucial our relationship to others really is.

Job 6:14-18

Those who withhold kindness from a friend forsake the fear of the Almighty. My companions are treacherous like a torrent-bed, like freshets that pass away, that run dark with ice, turbid with melting snow. In time of heat they disappear; when it is hot, they vanish from their place. The caravans turn aside from their course; they go up into the waste, and perish.

One translation renders that fourteenth verse: Friends should be kind to a despairing man, or he will give up faith in the Almighty.

Do you get the meaning of that? How you relate to and care about a person, and the way you express your concern, all support that person in his or her faith in God.

We never know who may be despairing. There are countless testimonies of people praying for others. We sometimes discover later that those for whom others were praying were going through great crisis. This can be so even with people we don't know. Often the biggest kindness we can show is in our praying.

Try to overcome the fact that you will never know the good that is done by your praying for strangers. Leave that to God, but trust the mystery "that more things are wrought by prayer than this world dreams of." Let persons call you to prayer. Prayer will call you to action.

Matthew 25:34-40

Then the king will say to those at his right hand, "Come, you that are blessed by my Father, inherit the kingdom prepared for you . . . for I was hungry and you gave me food, I was thirsty and you gave me something to drink, I was a stranger and you welcomed me, I was naked and you gave me clothing, I was sick and you took care of me, I was in prison and you visited me." Then the righteous will answer him, "Lord, when was it that we saw you hungry and gave you food, or thirsty and gave you something to drink? And when was it that we saw you a stranger and welcomed you, or naked and gave you clothing? And when was it that we saw you sick or in prison and visited you?" And the king will answer them, "Truly I tell you, just as you did it to one of the least of these who are members of my family, you did it to me."

Close this period today in the same fashion as yesterday, using whatever pattern of prayer is suitable to you. Take as much time as you need.

During the Day

You have three signals now: interruptions, situations, persons.

Let them all be the sounding gong in your soul which calls you to pray without ceasing today.

DAY FIVE

Attention

Exodus 3:1-5, RSV

Now Moses was keeping the flock of his father-in-law, Jethro, the priest of Midian; and he led his flock to the west side of the wilderness, and came to Horeb, the mountain of God. And the angel of the LORD appeared to him in a flame of fire out of the midst of a bush; and he looked, and lo, the bush was burning, yet it was not consumed. And Moses said, "I will turn aside and see this great sight, why the bush is not burnt." When the LORD saw that he turned aside to see, God called to him out of the bush, "Moses, Moses!" And he said, "Here am I." Then he said, "Do not come near; put off your shoes from your feet, for the place on which you are standing is holy ground."

I wonder what would have happened to Moses if he had not made the decision to "turn aside and see this great sight, why the bush is not burnt." The scripture says that it was after Moses "turned aside to see" that God called to him out of the bush.

Moses was doing his job in an ordinary sort of way. He wasn't in a church or at his special morning prayer time—just tending the flock of his father-in-law, business as usual. In the midst of that task he suddenly discovered something that he had never seen before, a bush aflame in an unusual way.

This *was* a unique visitation of God, dramatic, as we think about it. Yet there must be many "burning bushes" in our daily lives that we don't turn aside and see. Simone Weil, a Frenchwoman who died in 1943 at the age of thirty-three, became a kind of apostle of the spiritual life in France. Through her writings, which were published posthumously, she provided some keen insight about living prayer. Her definition of prayer as *attention* is on target. *Prayer is attention,* turning aside to see.

One of the greatest enemies, not only of prayer but of the whole spiritual life, is inattention—complacency. Pascal called this *the Gethsemane sleep*, referring to what the disciples did when Jesus asked them to watch with him.

Persons generally approach life in two ways, exercising two impulses: one, to accept and take for granted; two, to look with inquiring wonder. Moses responded with the latter impulse. He made the decision to leave his shepherd task for a moment, to turn aside from leading the sheep, to follow his curiosity and see what was going on. The burning bush caught his attention, and he decided to attend to what he saw.

The entire burning bush passage is vital to our understanding of prayer as attention—*seeing*, but also *attending* to what we see. Continuing with verse six, the passage relates: "And [God] said, 'I am the God of your father, the God of Abraham, the God of Isaac, and the God of Jacob.' And Moses hid his face, for he was afraid to look at God" (RSV).

Exodus 3:7-10:

Then the LORD said, "I have observed the misery of my people who are in Egypt; I have heard their cry on account of their taskmasters. Indeed, I know their sufferings, and I have come down to deliver them from the Egyptians, and to bring them up out of that land to a good and broad land, a land flowing with milk and honey. . . . The cry of the Israelites has now come to me; I have also seen how the Egyptians oppress them. So come, I will send you to Pharaoh to bring my people, the Israelites, out of Egypt."

Moses tried to argue with God—and prayer may involve that—offering excuses and begging God to send someone else. But eventually Moses responded and "took his wife and his sons, put them on a donkey and went back to the land of Egypt; and Moses carried the staff of God in his hand" (Exod. 4:20).

Paying attention is listening and responding to God's call. If Moses had never responded, he would never have been Moses; he would never have fulfilled his destiny.

I wrote of this in *Be Your Whole Self* as part of the process of "living deliberately."

It was when Moses *attended* to what he saw that God spoke to him. The height of the mystery is in Moses' response to this happening. He "hid his face, for he was afraid to look at God" (Exod. 3:6). The root of the word "mystery" is a Greek word meaning literally "to shut one's mouth." This is part of the "tuning in process"—to shut one's mouth that the Other might speak, to "take off one's shoes" for the ground is holy.[13]

This is at the heart of praying without ceasing: being attentive and attending to what we see. It is as we go beyond *looking* to *seeing* that we can consciously relate all of life to God. Then we begin to see God as "the beyond in the midst of life"; we know him not on the borders but at the center of life.

In a beautiful testimony of this, Tom and Edna Boone, leaders of LAOS, a volunteer mission organization headquartered in Washington, D.C., shared their experience in Mississippi before prayer became for them a matter of "paying attention."

> Life was good—simple and uncomplicated. We had been blessed by the arrival of our first child; we had lovely friends in the church who hardly ever disagreed with us, and we were working successfully with our youth as friends and counselors. Indeed, from our vantage point, it did truly seem that God was in His heaven and all was right with the world!
>
> What we could not seem to understand at that moment in history was that God was not in his heaven at all! He was starving to death in Calcutta and Lagos; he was rotting in prison in Bogotá and Sao Paulo; he was naked and sick in Big Stone Gap and Watts . . . and he was getting ready to march on Selma!"[14]

D. H. Lawrence defined thought as "a [person] in . . . wholeness, wholly attending." That's really what prayer is: in our wholeness, *in our image-of-God-wholeness*, wholly attending, consciously relating our life, and all of life, to God.

Reflecting and Recording

Yesterday you had three signals to call you to prayer: interruptions, situations, persons. These signals are all related to prayer as *attention*. Record here your prayer experience with:

1. Interruptions (List them and make notes about what your "Day by Day" prayer is meaning to you.)

2. Situations (What were the situations and how did you pray?)

3. Persons (Make notes describing your meetings with or the attention you gave persons, and how you prayed.)

Close this period today using the suggested morning or evening pattern suited to your time frame. It is hoped that your experience in situations and with persons yesterday will be part of your praying today. Your petitions, intercessions, seeking guidance, and thanksgiving may be directly related to the situations in which you were involved or the persons you encountered. Take as much time as you need.

During the Day

Prayer as attention is a matter of discipline. A part of the discipline is giving attention to our signals: interruptions, situations, persons. I hope that you are adding some signals of your own to make living prayer a reality. Concentrate today on "turning aside to see"—attending to situations and persons that may be your "burning bush."

DAY SIX

Awareness

Irenaeus, one of the fathers of the early church, captured in a poignant sentence a dimension of prayer: "The glory of God is man fully alive." The glory of God is not you on your knees, nor your pondering the Bible, nor you in the sanctuary caught up in the ecstasy of worship, nor your giving a cup of cold water to another. Not any one of these but maybe all of them—and a lot more. It is you and all humankind, fully alive.

This is what it means to pray without ceasing, to live our praying, to be alive—*aware*. Here is an understanding of prayer that makes praying without ceasing a viable possibility: *Prayer is awareness.*

There are four levels, or dimensions, of awareness that make us fully alive to the glory of God.

1. *Awareness of self*—being in touch with my own feelings. What's going on inside me?

2. *Awareness of others*—not just an acknowledgment that others exist but that they are alive. Not just being "with others" but "presencing" ourselves to them—being alive to them, sharing in their lives and allowing them to share in ours.

3. *Awareness of the world*—the world is not a prison from which we are to escape. Our flesh is not evil. The *world* is the house in which we who have been made *flesh* are to live. God made it all and saw that it was good.

4. *Awareness of God*—sensing the mystery, opening ourselves to the full expression of God's indwelling Spirit, being alive to God's action in others and the world.

The philosopher Martin Heidegger sees the condition of true knowledge to be "openness" to "what is." That is awareness, and that is the proper stance of living prayer: to be open to what is. This means an openness and acceptance of myself as I am, of others as they are, of God as God is, of the world as it is, to be open to what God wants to do through us and through others in the world.

Awareness is more natural for children than for adults. In the process of growth and aging we shut ourselves off from experiences, close our minds, become callous. Pain, embarrassment, sorrow, and failure train us to be selective in our experiencing. We build defenses against the possibility of what may be a negative or painful experience. So we close ourselves off from much of life. Many of us prefer the hell of a predictable situation rather than risk the joy of an unpredictable one. So we play it safe.

Awareness, then, is not natural for most of us. It must be cultivated. To be alive to life requires effort and discipline. We have to run risks and be open to what may mean hurt and failure. But the possibility for joy and meaning far outweighs the negative factors.

And who says that pain, embarrassment, sorrow, or failure are not as much a part of life as happiness, success, laughter, or confidence? The landscape of life is rather blah without the shadows. *The glory of God is each of us fully alive.*

A whole person—one fully alive—is in communion with one's self, with others, with God, and with the world. It may well be that one's communion with God is dependent upon communion with self, others, and the world!

Reflecting and Recording

To begin to discipline yourself in awareness, you need to look at where you are now. How aware are you? How alive?

On a scale of one to ten (ten being "fully alive"), rate yourself in awareness in the different areas. Simply put a check where you think you are today. If today is not typical for you—if something makes you feel unusually exhilarated, or if you are not feeling well—you may find it helpful to make two marks, one for today (√) and one (**X**) for your more normal awareness.

Awareness of Self

1 __   2 __   3 __   4 __   5 __   6 __   7 __   8 __   9 __   10 __

Awareness of Others

1 __   2 __   3 __   4 __   5 __   6 __   7 __   8 __   9 __   10 __

Awareness of the World

1 __   2 __   3 __   4 __   5 __   6 __   7 __   8 __   9 __   10 __

Awareness of God

1 __   2 __   3 __   4 __   5 __   6 __   7 __   8 __   9 __   10 __

Write two or three sentences about your assessment of yourself in these areas.

Awareness of Self:

Awareness of Others:

Awareness of the World:

Awareness of God:

Now close this period of reflecting and recording by thinking about this scripture as it relates to being alive. John's Gospel recalls Jesus saying:

John 15:9-16

"As the Father has loved me, so I have loved you; abide in my love. If you keep my commandments, you will abide in my love, just as I have kept my Father's commandments and abide in his love. I have said these things to you so that my joy may be in you, and that your joy may be complete.

"This is my commandment, that you love one another as I have loved you. No one has greater love than this, to lay down one's life for one's friends. You are my friends if you do what I command you. I do not call you servants any longer, because the servant does not know what the master is doing; but I have called you friends, because I have made known to you everything that I have heard from my Father. You did not choose me but I chose you. And I appointed you to go and bear fruit, fruit that will last, so that the Father will give you whatever you ask him in my name."

After reflecting on this scripture, close your period by using the guide to prayer you have used on previous days.

During the Day

Continue responding to the signals that call you to prayer. Be especially sensitive to how such responses enhance your awareness—make you come alive to yourself, to others, to the world, to God. Be joyful in this thought: "The glory of God is each of us fully alive!" (This is printed in large type on page 179. Cut it out, attach it to an index card, and place it on the kitchen table, your desk, or in some obvious place for your attention.)

DAY SEVEN

Praying and Living in Christ

There is a very simple prayer called "the Jesus Prayer" which can have tremendous meaning in your life. Some of the saints came to the point in their experience where, for long periods of time, they prayed only this prayer, "Lord Jesus Christ, Son of God, have mercy on me, a sinner."

Consider the vast meaning of this simple petition.

Lord Jesus Christ—what does it mean to call Jesus "Lord"?
Son of God—what does it mean to confess Jesus as the Son of God?
    What kind of God would give his Son in this fashion?
Have mercy—what does mercy mean? To utter the petition is to know
    that mercy is available. How do I claim that mercy?
Me, a sinner—what does that mean at this moment in my life?

Get in a relaxed position now, clear your mind, and center your thoughts on this one sentence: "Lord Jesus Christ, Son of God, have mercy on me, a sinner." If your mind picks up other thoughts and begins to wander, force your thinking back to this focus: "Lord Jesus Christ, Son of God, have mercy on me, a sinner." You may want to repeat it two or three times. Spend five minutes or so pondering the depth and meaning of this prayer for you today.

■ ■ ■

Based on your pondering write a sentence or two in response to the questions (listed above) related to the different dimensions of this prayer.
    Lord Jesus Christ

    Son of God

    Have mercy

    Me, a sinner

Now look at Jesus' words recorded in John's Gospel:

John 15:1-8

"I am the true vine, and my Father is the vinegrower. He removes every branch in me that bears no fruit. Every branch that bears fruit he prunes to make it bear more fruit. You have already been cleansed by the word that I have spoken to you. Abide in me as I abide in you. Just as the branch cannot bear fruit by itself unless it abides in the vine, neither can you unless you abide in me. I am the vine, you are the branches. Those who abide in me and I in them bear much

fruit, because apart from me you can do nothing. Whoever does not abide in me is thrown away like a branch and withers; such branches are gathered, thrown into the fire, and burned. If you abide in me, and my words abide in you, ask for whatever you wish, and it will be done for you. My Father is glorified by this, that you bear much fruit and become my disciples."

In another section (chapter 14) John has Jesus saying, "I will do whatever you ask in my name."

Paul's favorite description of a Christian was a person "in Christ." We cannot pray effectively without praying and living "in Christ."

Here is the secret of praying and living. Jesus came for one purpose: to bring himself to us, and in bringing himself to bring God. He came to give us power to do and be those things that God requires of us. "To all who received him . . . he gave power to become children of God" (John 1:12). Other noble martyrs and prophets gave us their words and their examples, but they could not give us the power to become like them. Only one has done that. We call him Savior and Lord!

At the heart of the good news is this truth that we must appropriate if we are to know the power of living prayer: Jesus as the Christ is alive. He is with us. In his resurrected power he is present with us. He loved the world and never left it. Jesus is among us now as much as when he lived among us in the flesh. Jesus invites us to accept the power of life he offers: "I am the true vine . . . . Abide in me, as I abide in you. . . . You are the branches. Those who abide in me and I in them bear much fruit" (John 15:1-5). "If you live your life in me, and my words live in your hearts, you can ask for whatever you like and it will come true for you" (John 15:7, PHILLIPS).

Until we grasp this or are grasped by it, we will not make much progress in Christian living and praying. When we know that we are guided by Christ, that he is the vine and we are the branches, we can claim power from the very Source of life to enliven, shape, change, and continually recreate us.

We live in Christ and we pray in Christ. The power is not in our praying, but in our living and praying in Christ. This is the thrilling lifetime adventure to which we are called. We can rest assured that what Jesus promises, he will provide. "Abide in me as I abide in you. Just as the branch cannot bear fruit by itself unless it abides in the vine, neither can you unless you abide in me. . . . Those who abide in me and I in them bear much fruit."

Reflecting and Recording

For seven days our emphasis has been on praying without ceasing. Hopefully you have begun something you will continue from now on: intentionally seeking consciously to relate all of life to God.

Has this effort made any difference in your life so far? Are you getting anywhere near the goal of praying without ceasing? Spend a few minutes reflecting on this. Write at least three or four sentences describing how you feel about this effort.

Christ is the vine; you and I are the branches. This means that we walk this day as God's own messengers. Whomever we meet, we meet in God's way. We are *with* every person and *in* every situation as the presence of Christ. Think about that. Write a few sentences about what that is going to mean to you today.

Close this time by praying in a manner of your choosing.

During the Day

Use "the Jesus prayer" for your interruptions today. Go back and review it to get it clearly in your mind.

Make this decision now: "I will either be Christ *to* or receive Christ *from* every person I meet today."

Group Meeting for Week Five

Introduction

Many do not pray because they do not understand prayer. They cannot rationally comprehend how prayer works, how God's power is released in our lives through our prayers and the prayers of others, or how our praying may empower and even bring change in other persons. It is a great day in our lives when, without complete understanding or rational explanation, we begin to practice prayer in an intentional, committed way.

There is a sense in which prayer, like many of the profound experiences of life, is absurd. Mystery is present—the holy! There are experiences like making a lifetime commitment to another person in marriage, being overwhelmed by great music, being made speechless by the grandeur of some piece of nature's handiwork, crying at the mystery of a birth or an act of self-sacrificing love, being moved to ecstatic joy or deep soul searching in worship. Such experiences may not make sense, and prayer is one of them. We pray because we must.

Enhancing this experience, turning all of life into a prayer, is what the discipline of praying is all about. This workbook is only an elemental introduction to the vast possibilities of living prayer. The possibilities unfold as we intentionally continue to pray.

You have made and are keeping a six-week commitment to this adventure. Knowing that many will want to continue the commitment, suggestions for a three-week extension are included in the Appendix (pages 175–77). At this meeting you may want to discuss this possibility, and those who wish may make a decision to extend their adventure. If you make that decision, the group leader for this week will look at the suggestions for continuation and will order the resources.

Sharing Together

1. Let each person share the "ingredient" of prayer that has become the most meaningful during these past two weeks.

2. Share your most meaningful experience of an interruption, situation, or person calling you to prayer.

3. Discuss the affirmation, "The glory of God is each of us fully alive."
   a. How did you come out in your self-rating of awareness? Talk about your needs in these particular areas (self, others, world, and God).
   b. What changes in your awareness level in any area have come as a result of this prayer adventure?
   c. Compare the four dimensions of awareness with the three arenas in which we operate as persons (private, institutional, group). In what ways is your prayer experience bringing these arenas together to enable you to function as a whole person with integrity?

4. "Many of us prefer the hell of a predictable situation rather than risk the joy of an unpredictable one."
   a. In what way has this statement been true in your experience?
   b. A faithful response to God may bring unpredictable results. Is anyone in the group wrestling with the anxiety of a call—some "burning bush" that is demanding attention—that you may wish to share with the group?

Praying Together

Before you begin your specific time of prayer, look at your group prayer list (if you made one last week). Do you need to delete some person, concern, or need, or add others? Be sensitive to answered prayer and to the need of committing some person or concern to God in faith, trusting God to act in each situation, and offering yourself as an instrument of God's redemptive love.

1. Begin your praying together with each person by saying "thank you" to God in a brief prayer of praise and thanksgiving. Do this in a few sentences—maybe

only one. For what are you thankful? What is happening in your life that is meaningful to you and brings you joy?

2. Last week we considered the possibilities of power in the human touch. We mentioned the specific practice of "laying on of hands."

    a. Are there persons who would like for the group to lay hands upon them and pray for them in a focused manner?

    b. Sometimes laying on of hands in *proxy* has great meaning. There may be a person or need on your group prayer list, or one that comes to your mind now, which one of you would like to represent in proxy, while others lay hands upon you and pray. The proxy person should clarify the need he or she represents as fully as possible. (If the name must be withheld, the person may identify the need.) The proxy person seeks to become one with the person for whom prayer is being offered.

3. A benediction is a blessing or greeting shared with another or with a group in parting. The "passing of the peace" is such a benediction. You take a person's hands and say, "The peace of God be with you," and the person responds, "And may God's peace be yours." Then that person, taking the hands of the person next to him or her, says, "The peace of God be yours," and receives the response, "And may God's peace be yours." Standing in a circle, let the leader "pass the peace," and let it go around the circle.

Week Six

Resources for Praying

INTRODUCTION
WEEK SIX

Our Power Depends on Our Prayer and Our Prayer Depends on Our Faith

One of the most breathtaking promises of Jesus is recorded in John 14:12-14:

> *Very truly, I tell you, the one who believes in me will also do the works that I do and, in fact, will do greater works than these, because I am going to the Father. I will do whatever you ask in my name, so that the Father may be glorified in the Son. If in my name you ask me for anything, I will do it.*

There are really two extravagant promises here. Jesus says, "Greater things than I have done will you do," and then he links that amazing word with his equally extravagant promise about prayer: "I will do whatever you ask in my name." He doesn't just say that once; he says it twice, obviously wanting it to register in our mind. Pay close attention to the verb tense: Jesus did not say, "I might do whatever you ask in my name." He didn't say, "I will probably do whatever you ask in my name." Nor did he say, "There's a good chance you will get whatever you ask in my name." No, he was emphatic: "I will do whatever you ask in my name."

Extravagant and unlimited, it seems, but we need to register the fact that the promise Jesus gives us here is not unconditional; rather, the promise is explicitly and strictly limited. It is only what we ask for "in Jesus' name," only what we pray "for his sake" that Jesus promises to give us.

We can confidently count on receiving what we ask, only if what we ask will advance God's cause and bring God glory.

Notice another connection and condition: The connection between faith and prayer. "He who *believes* in me will also do the works that I do." That's an underscoring of faith. So register this: Our power depends on our prayer, and our prayer depends on our faith. I've come to believe that the reason for the Christian's weakness is the weakness of the Christian's faith. One of my most moving prayer relationships was with Randy Morris, my wife's brother. Randy was forty years old when his world tumbled in. He, his wife Nancy, and their two children were living happily in Norfolk, Virginia. He had started his own business, something he had been dreaming of and planning for five years. Then it happened—double vision that took him to the doctor and an eventual diagnosis of lymphoma. The malignancy was in the spine, and there were tumors around the brain. Massive doses of chemotherapy put him in remission, and all rejoiced. But after about three months of remission the malignancy attacked again. Randy was tremendously depressed.

I had been preaching a series of sermons on the Psalms and I sent Randy copies of those sermons. Randy responded with a letter, a portion of which I share:

> Your prayers and the prayers of those you have asked to pray, such as David Libby's prayer group, have sustained me during those times when my personal prayer life was difficult (many occasions). A friend of mine with whom I meet weekly—you can call her my spiritual counselor—said that one of the most important dimensions of intercessory prayer is to uphold those when they find they cannot pray.

> I'm grateful for the two sermons you preached this summer. I have grown to love the Psalms during this past year. It is true that God does know of all our tossings.

> And now I will share with you a prayer experience that proves this to me. It was a major experience with Jesus. Father Rick and I have been touched in a way few people ever experience.

> For several years I have prepared for prayer by going through a total relaxation phase to release my body and mind for prayer. After a few moments I travel in my mind to a place in the north Georgia mountains where I used to go on camping trips. There I have built an open structure, a gazebo, where I go to talk with Jesus. Normally I go in and call for Jesus and he comes in. We visit, and usually I give him my prayers of thanksgiving and intercessions. It's a conversational sort of setting.

> In late August, I was completely demoralized with the recurrence of the lymphoma. I was an emotional wreck; I went into prayer. Everything went on as normal until Jesus came to the door of the gazebo. At that moment a completely unthought-of event happened that shook me to tears. I became like a camera recording the event. A little boy—myself—when I was about Evan's age (five years), ran up to Jesus and hugged him. He picked me up and carried me to a seat and held me in his arms. He hugged me. I didn't say anything, but he knew my "tossings." He knew I was frightened. There

were no answers and the future seemed so dim. As he hugged me he said, "Trust me. Trust me."

It was real, a personal miracle. He held me for a long time that night, until he knew I understood what he meant. I've told just a few people about this, and every time I tell it, even as I type this for you, tears come to my eyes; and the feeling I experienced that night renews itself in me. Rick said that feeling is "the same reason Moses couldn't look God in the face and why we remove our shoes on holy ground." And now I know that experience, too. We must trust Jesus as a child trusts—totally.

Because of this, whatever turns out to be the ultimate result of this disease, it's not the burden it was before. He made no promise, nor did he reveal the future, but he provided the format for living out the rest of my life with just two words . . . Trust me.

Well, Randy did this from that point on. He trusted Jesus. The difference it made in his life—the power of his witness—and the number of people he had ministered to all combined to tell a phenomenal story of what Jesus can do for a person.

My wife, Jerry, gave a bone-marrow transplant that extended his life for a year. Then Randy died. Not long before his death, he wrote me a letter that included this paragraph:

But the healing will be deeper than that (i.e., physical healing). There will be full reconciliation within my spirit and soul such as I have never enjoyed before. I truly feel the words written in *The Book of Common Prayer* about reconciliation: "Now there is rejoicing in heaven; for you were lost, and are found; you were dead, and are now alive in Christ Jesus our Lord. Go in peace. The Lord has put away all your sins. Thanks be to God."

Randy provided a powerful witness to the integration of prayer into the life of spiritual wholeness and Christian witness. During this last week you will be looking at some resources for prayer. Randy's model is one that you might want to explore. Above all, the lesson Randy learned is the lesson we must learn about all of life, and prayer is a key teacher. This lesson is Jesus' invitation that says, "Trust me."

DAY ONE

"Put Yourself in the Presence of God"

Colossians 1:23-27, PHILLIPS (1960 edition)

I myself have been made a minister of this same Gospel, and though it is true at this moment that I am suffering on behalf of you who have heard the Gospel, yet I am far from sorry about it. Indeed, I am glad, because it gives me a chance to complete in my own sufferings something of the untold pains which Christ suffers on behalf of his body, the Church. For I am a minister of the Church by divine commission, a commission granted to me for your benefit and for a special purpose: that I might fully declare God's word—that sacred mystery which up till now has been hidden in every age and every generation, but which is now as clear as daylight to those who love God. They are those to whom God has planned to give a vision of the full wonder and splendor of his secret plan for [the nations]. And the secret is simply this: Christ in you! Yes, Christ in you bringing with him the hope of all the glorious things to come.

Sit quietly for two or three minutes with this verse of scripture at the center of your thinking: "The secret is simply this: Christ *in you!* Yes, Christ *in you* bringing with him the hope of all the glorious things to come."

■ ■ ■

Jesus was clear about one rule of prayer: "When you pray, go into a room by yourself, shut the door, and pray to your Father who is there in the secret place" (Matt. 6:6, NEB). In seeking a life of living prayer, there must be those times (and most of us need them daily) when we deliberately put ourselves in the presence of God. This is the time when we stop being "too elsewhere" and are there—there in our room, door shut, alone with God.

This does not mean that we have to be in a given room at a given time performing some established ritual of prayer. It does mean that we want to commune with God greatly enough that we will find a time and a place to give ourselves in an act of receptivity to God, that we will seek consciously to open ourselves to God, allowing God to influence our minds, hearts, and wills.

This six-week adventure in living prayer is a practice run (dress rehearsal) for what can become an ongoing pattern for you. In this last week of our workbook venture, we are exploring some possible resources for praying, resources that will enhance and enrich your "alone with God" period.

Today the focus is on the beginning of your "alone with God" time. The saints of the ages who have described their prayer patterns invariably begin with a common exercise: In one way or another they deliberately put themselves in the presence of God. Most of the great men and women of prayer have insisted that our prayer in secret must be formal at the start.

As we considered last week, this is a matter of *attention*. But now our attention is focused on a definite period of prayer. Simone Weil reminds us that prayer is attention. It is the orientation of all the attention of which the soul is capable toward God.

Many people find that a particular place for daily prayer is an invaluable aid. When my children were growing up, I found I could focus my attention better in my study than any place else. Now that my children are gone, my place of prayer is in our living room. We have a window seat behind the sofa. There I keep a Bible, the books I'm currently using for devotional reading, and a pad and pen for making notes. For you, it may be that a comfortable chair in the den or living room or bedroom will be your place, your "closet." I know a businessman who has a chair in the corner of his office where he makes his rendezvous with God.

The point is that many of us need a place to which we come in deliberate fashion. We are coming to "meet" God. In an act of commitment, we turn our attention to God. How we focus our attention varies from person to person. It may or may not affect our *feeling*. It really is a matter of *will*.

Here I am, Lord. I am here to meet you. I acknowledge your presence. I am going to spend this time with you. Help me to realize that I am *in your presence*, you are with me, even though I may not feel your presence.

Some people find it helpful as they settle in their place to begin their time alone with God by praying (sometimes silently, sometimes aloud) the Lord's Prayer.

Currently, this is my practice: I get up at six o'clock and put a pot of coffee on. I go to my place in the living room; and I simply sit there in quietness, reminding myself that I am meeting God there. Then I read a selection from the writings of Hannah Whitall Smith, a book entitled *God Is Enough*. It is an effective way of focusing my attention on what that period of time is all about. I am going to be *intentionally* with God. After that, I pray in a very specific way—including my intercession for others.

By then the coffee is ready; I get a cup of coffee, come back to my place, and begin to read the scripture. I am currently using an edition of the Bible that is arranged in such a way that you read through the entire Bible in a year. A portion of each day's reading includes a reading from the Hebrew Scriptures and the New Testament, a psalm, and a few verses from Proverbs. I reflect on the meaning of this scripture for my own life, and I close with another period of specific prayer, committing my life—especially that particular day—and my relationships to the Lord.

Off and on through the years, I return to an exercise that is very meaningful to me. When I go to my place of devotion, reminding myself that I am there to meet

God, I stand erect and begin to breathe deeply and to exhale completely. I try to get in control of my body by breathing. Then I enter into a devotional breathing exercise. As I breathe in deeply, I say to myself, "The secret is simply this: Christ in you!" I hold my breath as I say further to myself, "Yes, Christ in me." Then I exhale completely as I finish this affirmation of scripture: "bringing with him the hope of all the glorious things to come."

I repeat this deep rhythmic breathing a number of times. There's nothing magical about this kind of exercise; I just find that not only do I get my body under control through breathing—I get my mind focused in attention to Christ through immersing myself in this great affirmation, claiming his presence within me.

You will find your own way in focusing attention, because unless prayer begins with *attention*—deliberately putting yourself in the presence of God—it is not likely to begin.

Reflecting and Recording

Experiment with this devotional breathing exercise. First, go back and read the entire passage of scripture printed at the beginning of this session.

Stand up now and breathe deeply, hold your breath a moment, then exhale completely. Do it rhythmically now as you fill your mind with these thoughts:

Breathing in: "The secret is simply this, Christ in me!"
Holding breath: "Yes, Christ in me."
Exhaling: "Bringing with him the hope of all the glorious things to come."

When you have repeated this breathing pattern a number of times, settle down in a relaxed position and continue your prayer period in whatever fashion is meaningful to you.

During the Day

If you haven't done so by now, get this verse of scripture solidly in your mind. Clip it from page 179 to carry with you today.

The secret is simply this: Christ in you! Yes, Christ in you bringing with him the hope of all the glorious things to come.

During the day when you are tired, uptight, frustrated, weary, uncertain, or confused, stop whatever you are doing and perform this breathing exercise to the rhythm of this verse of scripture. Not only will you regain control of your physical self and perspective, you will be filled with the power and certainty of the indwelling Christ.

Don't forget the Jesus prayer: "Lord Jesus Christ, Son of God, have mercy on me, a sinner." Continue to use this in your interruptions.

Yesterday you were asked to make this decision: "I will either be Christ *to* or receive Christ *from* every person I meet today." Renew that decision and act upon it today.

DAY TWO

"Not by Bread Alone"

For two days you have been asked either to be Christ or to receive Christ from every person you met. Did you respond to that? If so, record here some things that happened as a result of that deliberate effort.

What about the devotional-breathing exercise? Did you have occasion to try it? Note here the results.

John Wesley once wrote, "Whether you like it or no, read and pray daily. It is for your life; there is no other way; else you will be a trifler all your days. . . . Do justice to your soul; give it time and means to grow. Do not starve yourself any longer."[15]

Matthew 4:1-4

Then Jesus was led by the Spirit up into the wilderness to be tempted by the devil. He fasted forty days and nights, and afterwards he was famished. The tempter came and said to him, "If you are the Son of God, command these stones to become loaves of bread." But he answered, "It is written 'One does not live by bread alone, but by every word that comes from the mouth of God.'"

Deuteronomy 8:1-3

This entire commandment that I command you today you must diligently observe, so that you may live and increase, and go in and occupy the land that the LORD promised on oath to your ancestors. Remember the long way that the LORD your God has led you these forty years in the wilderness, in order to humble you, testing you to know what was in your heart, whether or not you would keep his commandments. He humbled you by letting you hunger, then by feeding you with manna, with which neither you nor your ancestors were acquainted, in order to make you understand that one does not live by bread alone, but by every word that comes from the mouth of the LORD.

Jesus was equipped to deal with the devil in the wilderness. He had done justice to his soul, having lived with the scripture. So when, in his gnawing hunger, the temptation of turning stones into bread came, Jesus' mind went back to the wilderness trek of his forefathers and the lesson God had taught: "One does not live by bread alone."

By including scripture as part of our daily adventure, I have been saying implicitly what I want to make explicit now: *Scripture is a primary resource for praying.* It is impossible for me to imagine that we can develop a meaningful life of prayer without living with the scripture.

There are many ways to read and study the Bible. Our focus here is on reading the Bible as part of our praying. Such reading, while informed by our best understanding of scripture, should not be laborious or primarily critical. (There is a place for critical study.) Rather, we need to read expectantly. Believe that through the Bible God is going to speak to you. Come to your reading with the sense that you are entering the land of the Spirit. People of God have shared their venture of faith, and now you are journeying with them. Be *expectant* about the discoveries you will make.

Deliberately put yourself into it. Keep asking, "Is it I?" Be ready for revelation. Let what you read search, even accuse. Let it comfort and heal. Accept the challenge or guidance that is for you.

Test it by Jesus. The Bible is the record of men and women groping for God, their struggle to be God's people, their fumbling and growing in understanding of who God is and what God expected of them. Jesus is our revelation of God and our guide to full humanity under God. So we need to use our best understanding of the scripture to find out who this Jesus is, what he taught, and how those teachings were appropriated at the time. We need to immerse ourselves in this Jesus, to live with him as he is witnessed to and shared in the New Testament. We test the total witness of the Bible by him.

Remember that the Bible belongs to human life. It came out of the experience of flesh and blood, the dark problems of human existence and the bright light of divine-human communion. Thus it is the word of God through humans, for humans.

In using the scripture as a prayer resource, we should read by thought, incident, or lesson. Don't be intent on reading an entire chapter or an entire book. Read for the message. It may be a few verses or many.

For your reflection today stay with the bread theme by considering a passage from John.

John 6:30-40

So they said to him, "What sign are you going to give us then, so that we may see it and believe you? What work are you performing? Our ancestors ate the manna in the wilderness; as it is written, 'He gave them bread from heaven to eat.'" Then Jesus said to them, "Very truly, I tell you, it was not Moses who gave you the bread from heaven, but it is my Father who gives you the true bread from heaven. For the bread of God is that which comes down from heaven and gives life to the world." They said to him, "Sir, give us this bread always."

Jesus said to them, "I am the bread of life. Whoever comes to me will never be hungry, and whoever believes in me will never be thirsty. But I said to you that you have seen me and yet do not believe. Everything that the Father gives me will come to me, and anyone who comes to me I will never drive away; for I have come down from heaven, not to do my own will, but the will of him who sent me. And this is the will of him who sent me, that I should lose nothing of all that he has given me, but raise it up on the last day. This is indeed the will of my Father, that all who see the Son and believe in him may have eternal life; and I will raise them up on the last day."

Reflecting and Recording

Experiment again with the method of discovery you used on Day Three of last week in reflecting upon the above passage of scripture. You may want to read it again.

1. What does the scripture say? While all reading involves interpretation, don't let that obscure what is actually in the text. Simply try to hear what is said. Record in your own words here.

2. What does the scripture mean to you right now? What is Jesus trying to say? Try to interpret, to discover the meaning behind the words.

Note: Through the ages, Christians have found it helpful to test their interpretations of scripture against the interpretations the Spirit has given to the whole community. You, too, may wish to tell your understanding of the scripture with others sharing this adventure with you.

3. If you decided to act upon the message of this scripture, what would that mean? Would there be any changes in your life? What changes? If you accept this word as Jesus' word to you today, what would you have to do in response? Write your answers here.

Move to a brief time of deliberate prayer. You may wish to use the devotional-breathing exercise suggested yesterday. Then settle down in a relaxed position and continue your prayer period in whatever fashion is meaningful to you. Your experience with the scripture will probably become the focus of your praying.

During the Day

Continue to use "the Jesus Prayer" in your interruptions.

Look at your home library and see how many different translations of the Bible you have. If you don't have a good modern translation (*New Revised Standard, New King James, Phillips, New English Bible, New International Version,* or *Good News Bible*), then treat yourself today. If you cannot find one in a local bookstore, order one from your church publishing house. If you want to have a big treat, secure a copy of the New Testament or the entire Bible in a number of different versions. Commonly one volume will include only four versions. (You can select a volume that includes some of your favorite translations.) You may have to order this through your church publishing house.

The purpose behind using different translations is not to find one that lends itself to what you would like it to say, but to expose yourself to different possibilities of having God address you through the scriptures. Sometimes this is an assuring experience; sometimes it makes us face things we don't want to hear. Since we trust God's goodness, we can open ourselves to whatever God would say to us.

If you did not have the occasion to try the devotional breathing exercise during the day yesterday, keep the possibility in mind for today. If you did, and another occasion for its use arises today, try it.

DAY THREE

"Being Quiet before the Word"

Imagination and meditation are great resources for praying. Entire books have been written on meditation as well as on mental prayer. In this workbook, I simply want to introduce a possibility for the use of imagination and meditation with scripture as a meaningful way to enhance a life of prayer.

Here are guidelines for this manner of praying:

1. *Center down, deliberately placing yourself in the presence of God.* We considered this first step in prayer on Day One of this week. (You may want to review it.)

2. *Be quiet before the Word.* Select a passage of scripture (the parables of Jesus especially lend themselves to this approach). Read the passage slowly, giving it your full attention.

3. *Be passively open.* Don't try to figure things out, but be open to leading and suggestion. Don't try to impose your rationalization or logic on the scripture at this point.

4. *Deliberately focus your mind on the scripture.* Let your imagination become active, cooperating with God in becoming aware of whatever thoughts or feelings come from the content of the scripture you are considering. This cooperation may take many forms. Honest struggling and searching are signs of your willingness and sincerity to hear God's word addressed to you. When you do find yourself struggling over a tough or obscure saying, make sure it's a cooperative struggling!

5. *Listen to the scripture speaking to you.* Try to imagine what you would feel if you were one of the persons in the scripture. Try to get in touch with your own feelings as you respond to the action or relationships or attitudes present in the scripture with which you are living.

6. *Make whatever application to your life that seems appropriate.* Deal with the feelings that come.

Here is a brief example:

Luke 18:10-14

Two men went up to the temple to pray, one a Pharisee and the other a tax collector. The Pharisee, standing by himself, was praying thus, "God, I thank you that I am not like other people: thieves, rogues, adulterers, or even like this tax collector. I fast twice a week; I give a tenth of all my income." But the tax collector, standing far off, would not even look up to heaven, but was beating his breast and saying, "God, be merciful to me, a sinner!" I tell you, this man went down to his home justified rather than the other; for all who exalt themselves will be humbled, but all who humble themselves will be exalted.

My Response

I want to be a somebody! I am somebody, but I have not always known that. What did Jesus mean? "Everyone who sets himself up as a somebody will become a nobody."

Somebody and *nobody* are big words for me—too big. Coming out of poverty and cultural deprivation, I've struggled with that "somebody/nobody" business. Deep resentments have been gnawing away at my life, my personhood. Much of my life has been spent trying to be what I thought was a *somebody*, trying to prove to people that I was not a *nobody*.

Even though I have my past in perspective and I've overcome my resentments, I still fall back into the snare. I sometimes want to stand in the middle of the crowd and say, "See here, I've made it; I am worthy of your acceptance; I've proved myself." Is that what was going on with the Pharisee? He had worked hard at his religion. I've worked hard at mine. I've tried to be good—I've *been* good. I can't say I'm not greedy as he could, because I do find myself grasping at *things*. I'm honest. I'm pure—not always pure in my thinking and attitudes, but pure in my overt acts, at least most of the time. I tithe. I pray. I even fast sometimes! That ought to mean something. Yeah! I can identify with that Pharisee in the middle of the temple.

The tax collector over in the corner—I can identify with him too. Not in the same way of being a blatant sinner begging God for mercy but crying out for some sign of God's presence. I'm caught—or I feel I am. I don't want to be religious like that Pharisee; but in my particular ministry, people are wanting to put me in a mold of righteousness—I feel they are expecting more spiritual power from me than I possess. I go somewhere to teach about prayer, and people want a "giant of the spirit" to stand among them and show them how to pray. I want to slink over in a corner and pray for mercy for myself. And I do!

I guess I'm somewhere between the Pharisee and the tax collector. I want to be *somebody*. I don't want to be a *nobody*. I am somebody. I hear you, Jesus! Being somebody and pretending to be somebody are two different things. The somebody I am will keep on resisting the efforts of people to make a phony *spiritual giant* out of me. The somebody I am will continue to feel my need for mercy and perspective. The somebody I am will continue to be the somebody who gets my identity and sense of self-worth from what I am inside and the wholeness I feel. I'll be humble in my relationship to you and to others—at least I will try to be! I won't exalt myself or try to prove myself. I'll try to be one of your unique somebodies among all the somebodies of the world. I'll keep trying never to think of another as a *nobody*.

Reflecting and Recording

Go back now and review the guidelines, and apply them to your consideration of the familiar parable of the prodigal son. Be quiet in the way that has been suggested and illustrated.

Luke 15:11-32

Then Jesus said, "There was a man who had two sons. The younger of them said to his father, 'Father, give me the share of the property that will belong to me.' So he divided his property between them. A few days later the younger son gathered all he had and traveled to a distant country, and there he squandered his property in dissolute living. When he had spent everything, a severe famine took place throughout that country, and he began to be in need. So he went and hired himself out to one of the citizens of that country, who sent him to his fields to feed the pigs. He would gladly have filled himself with the pods that the pigs were eating; and no one gave him anything. But when he came to himself he said, 'How many of my father's hired hands have bread enough and to spare, but here I am dying of hunger! I will get up and go to my father, and I will say to him, "Father, I have sinned against heaven and before you; I am no longer worthy to be called your son; treat me like one of your hired hands."' So he set off and went to his father. But while he was still far off, his father saw him and was filled with compassion; he ran and put his arms around him and kissed him. Then the son said to him, 'Father, I have sinned against heaven and before you; I am no longer worthy to be called your son.' But the father said to his slaves, 'Quickly, bring out a robe—the best one—and put it on him; put a ring on his finger and sandals on his feet. And get the fatted calf and kill it, and let us eat and celebrate; for this son of mine was dead and is alive again; he was lost and is found!' And they began to celebrate.

"Now his elder son was in the field; and when he came and approached the house, he heard music and dancing. He called one of the slaves and asked what was going on. He replied, 'Your brother has come, and your father has killed the fatted calf, because he has got him back safe and sound.' Then he became angry and refused to go in. His father came out and began to plead with him. But he answered his father, 'Listen! For all these years I have been working like a slave for you, and I have never disobeyed your command; yet you have never given me even a young goat so that I might celebrate with my friends. But when this son of yours came back, who has devoured your property with prostitutes, you killed the fatted calf for him!' Then the father said to him, 'Son, you are always with me, and all that is mine is yours. But we had to celebrate and rejoice, because this brother of yours was dead and has come to life; he was lost and has been found.'"

My Response (Write your response here.)

During the Day

Once before you were asked to share with someone who is not part of this adventure what this experience is meaning to you. Do that again today—maybe with the same person (if you can remember), bringing that person up to date on where you are in this experience. You may want to share with more than one if the occasion arises, but at least share with one.

Continue to use your signals to call you to prayer.

DAY FOUR

Praying the Psalms

Another rich resource for praying is the Psalms. The Psalms were used as the "prayer book" of ancient Israel and, no doubt, by Jesus. Jesus died with a psalm on his lips and, I'm sure, with a psalm in his heart.

I come back to this resource often, and my plan is simple. I begin at the first psalm, and I read until a particular psalm grabs me, until some fire is sparked in my soul. I reflect upon it and let it get into my mind. I make it my own and relate it to where I am at that particular time in my life.

The next day I begin where I left off on the previous day. I read until my mind stands at attention before some relevant thought or truth. I continue that process until I have finished the Psalms. I lay the Psalms aside and turn to some other resource. I have returned to the Psalms at other times to find, on another journey through them, that other fires are sparked from different psalms than in previous readings.

I usually write my prayers and responses to these psalms in a kind of spiritual diary. I find I can go back and read the thoughts, feelings, and prayers of previous days as a resource for my praying now.

Here is a sample. In one of my journeys I came to Psalm 19 and began to read:

Psalm 19:1-9

The heavens are telling the glory of God;
    and the firmament proclaims his handiwork.
Day to day pours forth speech,
    and night to night declares knowledge.
There is no speech, nor are there words;
    their voice is not heard;
yet their voice goes out through all the earth,
    and their words to the end of the world.
In the heavens he has set a tent for the sun,
    which comes out like a bridegroom
        from his wedding canopy,
    and like a strong man runs its course with joy.
Its rising is from the end of the heavens,
    and its circuit to the end of them;
    and nothing is hid from its heat.
The law of the LORD *is perfect,*
    reviving the soul;
the decrees of the LORD *are sure,*
    making wise the simple;
the precepts of the LORD *are right,*
    rejoicing the heart;
the commandment of the LORD *is clear,*
    enlightening the eyes;
the fear of the LORD *is pure,*
    enduring forever;
the ordinances of the LORD *are true,*
    and righteous altogether.

(On another journey these were the words that had caught my attention: *the law, precepts, commandment, fear,* and *ordinances of the Lord*—but not this particular morning. I read on.)

Psalm 19:10-13

More to be desired are they than gold,
    even much fine gold;

sweeter also than honey
    and drippings of the honeycomb.
Moreover by them is your servant warned;
    in keeping them there is great reward.
But who can detect their errors?
    Clear me from hidden faults.
Keep back your servant also from [proud thoughts];
    do not let them have dominion over me.
Then I shall be blameless,
    and innocent of great transgression.

I was stopped short, almost abruptly. The words began to turn in my mind.

But who can detect their errors?
    Clear me from hidden faults.
Keep back your servant also from [proud thoughts];
    do not let them have dominion over me.

After living with that for a while, letting it tumble around in my mind and heart, I wrote in my diary:

Lord, this is where I am, this is my need.
Just last night Jerry (my wife) reminded me
of how I hurt her earlier in the day.
A friend had come; we were excited.
Conversation flowed like a rushing stream.
But I "hogged" it!
Twice Jerry tried to share from the depths of herself,
wanting to bring Gary up to date on her own pilgrimage.
Twice I had cut her off, not allowing her to
share, so intent upon myself.
I didn't know I had done it
until she courageously confronted me with it.
Thank you, God, for her courage!
She confronted me
only after I made what I thought was a perceptive comment
about another couple who were with us:
"They certainly are out of touch with each other—
don't seem to be communicating at all—
just talking past each other."
She couldn't stifle her hurt
so she told me of my calloused blundering.
O Lord, clear me of hidden faults.
I saw the *splinter* in my friends' eyes

but was unaware of the *beam* in my own.
Keep back your servant also from [proud thoughts],
do not let them have dominion over me.
I am so presumptuous, Lord.
Forgive me.

I shared my prayer experience with Jerry that same day. So, not only did I ask God's forgiveness for my hidden faults and proud thoughts, I sought to make amends with my wife for my callousness.

Reflecting and Recording

It constantly amazes me that almost every day I find the trigger for my reflection, confession, affirmation, thanksgiving, intercession, and celebration in the Psalms. I believe you will find it so. Try it.

1. Turn your Bible to the Psalms. Begin reading with the first psalm. Read until something demands your attention. Record here the portion of the psalm on which you focus.

Now let the words come alive in your mind. Think about them. What do these words mean to you now? Live with them for awhile.

■ ■ ■

2. Then write your response here—maybe as a prayer, maybe just as an expression of feeling.

During the Day

Pick out one verse or section of the psalm you have been considering and memorize it. If you don't have time to memorize it, write it on a piece of paper and take it with you during the day. Consider it often to remind you of this experience.

DAY FIVE

"Soak Your Soul in the Great Models"

Begin in the Psalms where you left off yesterday. Read until you come to the thoughts, feelings, and petitions that speak for you today. Record those verses here.

Let these verses ferment in your mind. What do they mean to you now? Ponder your response for a few minutes.

■ ■ ■

In 1974 I had only recently come to my ministry with The Upper Room, seeking to inspire, motivate, and provide resources for people to recover a vital life of prayer. I had the opportunity to spend a couple of hours with Elton Trueblood, one of the great examples and interpreters of Christian living in our time. Dr. Trueblood is a Quaker, thus coming from a rich heritage of prayer and personal piety. I asked Dr. Trueblood, "If you were given this assignment for ministry, how would you go about it; what would you do?"

Among the many things he said, this one still stands out: "However you do it, Maxie, try to motivate people to soak their souls in the great models. Get them to live with the saints, the classic books of prayer and spiritual pilgrimage."

On the elevator, going to my room on another floor in the hotel where both Dr. Trueblood and I were staying that day, I was certain that what he said was true. As I reflected upon it, as a witness confirming the truth of it, the words of Frank Laubach, one of those modern models in whom we need to "soak our souls," came vividly to my mind:

I climbed "Signal Hill" back of my house talking and listening to God all the way up, all the way back, all the lovely half hour on the top. And God talked back! . . . Below me lay the rice fields, and as I looked across them,

I heard my tongue saying aloud, "Child, just as the rice needs the sunshine every day, and could not grow if it had sun only once a week or one hour a day, so you need me all day of every day. People over all the world are withering because they are open toward God only rarely. Every waking minute is not too much."

A few months ago I was trying to write a chapter on "the discovering of God." Now that I have discovered [God] I find that it is a continuous discovery. Every day is rich with new aspects of [God] and [God's] working. As one makes new discoveries about [God's] friends by being with them, so one discovers the "individuality" of God if one entertains [God] continuously. One thing I have seen this week is that God loves beauty. Everything [God] makes is lovely. The clouds, the tumbling river, the waving lake, the soaring eagle, the slender blade of grass, the whispering of the wind, the fluttering butterfly—this graceful transparent nameless child of the lake which clings to my window for an hour and vanishes forever. Beautiful craft of God! And I know that [God] makes my thought-life beautiful when I am open all the day to [God]. If I throw these mind-windows apart and say, "God, what shall we think of now?" [God] answers always in some graceful, tender dream.

And I know that God is love-hungry, . . . constantly pointing me to some dull, dead soul which [God] has never reached and wistfully urges me to help [God] reach that stolid, tight-shut mind. O God, how I long to help You with these (Maranaws). And with these Americans! And with these Filipinos! All day I see souls dead to God look sadly out of hungry eyes. I want them to know my discovery! That any minute can be paradise, that any place can be heaven! That [anyone] can have God! That [everyone] does have God the moment he [or she] speaks to God, or listens for [God]![16]

I had committed that letter to memory years before when, as a young minister just out of seminary in my first parish, I was making some deliberate, though fumbling, steps on my prayer pilgrimage. It had been years since I had specifically lived with the classics and great models of prayer. I had moved on to what I thought were more modern, more relevant expressions, but the depth of these experiences was still imprinted on my soul. I could still quote much of the passage from memory.

At the close of the workbook is a list of resources we can use to "soak our souls in the great models." Many of these books are in paperback and thus are inexpensive and available to everyone.

A friend gave me *The Joy of the Saints* as a Christmas gift in 1992. It is a collection of spiritual readings from the "saints"—a reading for each day of the year. I have been using it in my devotional periods during 1993. Before I began working on this new revision of *The Workbook of Living Prayer*, I read the October 1 selection from *The Joy of the Saints*. It begins with this sentence from Thérèse of Lisieux: "It is God's will here below that we shall distribute to one another by prayer the treasures with which [God] has enriched us." I cannot get that sentence out of my mind. It's a new thought for me—the meaning of which I have not yet appropriated—but what a challenging consideration: Through our praying we distribute to one another the "treasures" with which God has enriched us.

Another powerful truth to ponder from *The Joy of the Saints* is the reading for September 30 from Augustine: "We believe, not because we know but so that we may come to know." I share this update from my own experience simply to underscore the rich resources the great models provide.

Reflecting and Recording

"Soak your soul" for four or five minutes in this great prayer of Saint Francis of Assisi, one of the great models: "I beseech Thee, O Lord, that the fiery and sweet strength of Thy love may absorb my soul from all things that are under heaven, and I may die for love of Thy love as Thou didst deign to die for the love of my love."[17]

■ ■ ■

Now put in your own words a prayer that would express the same desire as that of Saint Francis. Write your prayer here.

During the Day

Look at the list of classics at the close of this workbook. Do you have one of them in your home library? If so, take a look at it sometime today. Maybe you would like to start reading one of them.

If you don't have any of these, call your church or public library. Chances are you will find some of them. Check one out to peruse in the days ahead.

Continue seeking consciously to relate all of life to God by using the signals that are meaningful to you.

DAY SIX

"Singing the Lord's Song"

Here are the first three verses of Psalm 88:

O LORD, God of my salvation,
    when, at night, I cry out in
        your presence,
let my prayer come before you;
    incline your ear to my cry.
For my soul is full of troubles,
    and my life draws near to
        Sheol.

Here are the first two verses of Psalm 89:

I will sing of your steadfast love,
    O LORD, forever;
    with my mouth I will proclaim
        your faithfulness to all generations.
I declare that your steadfast love
    is established forever;
    your faithfulness is as firm as
        the heavens.

The states of mind and the moods of the psalmist praying are in dramatic contrast. In Psalm 88 a person whose "soul" is full of troubles cries out to the Lord. Psalm 89 is a song of joy to God whose faithfulness the psalmist has experienced "as firm as the heavens" and whose "steadfast love is established forever." Both psalms are the honest expressions of a person in prayer, waiting on the Lord, sharing the depths of one's soul.

The psalmist was not without words to express those feelings. Sometimes I am without words, and thus I've discovered a source of praying that is enriching my life. I discovered it about eight years ago, so it was not included in the original *Workbook of Living Prayer*. I don't know why it took me so long. Many guides to prayer, such as *A Guide to Prayer for Ministers and Other Servants* by Rueben P. Job and Norman Shawchuck, and its sequel, *A Guide to Prayer for All God's People,* include a hymn for each day. But I never thought about singing those hymns; I read the words.

I was going through a dry spell in my prayer life, and confessed this to a person with whom I was counseling. He was surprised that I would share with him my own struggle. What happens so often when we are open and vulnerable to each other is that ministry flows in both directions. This fellow said, "Let me tell you what I do when I can't pray." Then he said that the founding pastor of the congregation I serve, Christ United Methodist Church in Memphis, Dr. Charles Grant, had suggested this to him years ago. "I sing," he said. "I sing some of the hymns that I know by memory." And then he added with a wry smile, "Why don't you try it?"

Well I did, and it's been a wonderful experience.

I use this resource of singing specifically when two extreme kinds of things are going on in my life. One, when my joy and happiness are so rich and full that I can't find words to express my gratitude to God, I sing. Two, when I'm numb, dull, dry. I also sing when I'm desperate, confused, or frustrated.

I have a hymn book in my place of morning prayer and devotion. Sometimes I may simply thumb through the hymnbook and find a hymn that invites me to sing it. But more often than not, I simply sing from memory. Twenty years ago when I first wrote this workbook, had I been using the resource of singing I would have been singing the great hymns of the church and some of the gospel hymns that I learned in the country church of my childhood. I still sing those on occasion, but more often than not I'm singing some of the more contemporary praise music that has come through the church. The two that I probably sing more often than any others are these:

I love you, Lord, and I lift my voice to worship you; O my soul, rejoice.
Take joy, my King, in what you hear; may it be a sweet, sweet sound in your ear.

I sing this when I simply want to praise God for who God is and what God is doing. The other is this:

Jesus, Jesus, Jesus! There's just something about that name!
Master, Savior, Jesus! Like the fragrance after the rain.
Jesus, Jesus, Jesus! Let all heaven and earth proclaim:
Kings and kingdoms will all pass away,
But there's something about that name!

When I'm desperate or feeling pain and confusion, and am unable to focus or to clarify my thoughts and feelings or to utter any words, I just sing that Jesus hymn and it becomes my prayer. Earlier in the workbook we talked about praying in Jesus' name and the power of Jesus' name. This is a vivid example of it for me. Just to center my heart on Jesus by singing becomes a transforming experience. And I simply trust the Lord to take that expression as the heart cry of that which is going on within me, or as Paul says, "Sighs too deep for words."

There is another dimension to this as well. We have a picture of it in Psalm 137. The children of Israel were in exile in Babylon. They found themselves there, not as willing tourists but as the unwilling spoils of battle. They were in exile in a land that had nothing but contempt for God. When one of those exiles returned years later and reflected on his experience, he wrote these words that are among the most touching in the Bible:

Psalm 137:1-3

By the rivers of Babylon—
    there we sat down and there
        we wept
        when we remembered Zion.
On the willows there
    we hung up our harps.
For there our captors
    asked us for songs,
and our tormentors asked for
        mirth, saying,
        "Sing us one of the songs of
            Zion!"

When that request was made of them—"Sing us one of the songs of Zion"—the psalmist asked the probing question, "How could we sing the Lord's song in a foreign land?" But Israel did precisely that—throughout their history. They sang the Lord's song. So in the foreign lands of our devotional experience as well as in our actual life, singing can be a great source of testifying to our faith, reminding us of who we are and whose we are, and linking us with the community of faith that through the centuries has maintained courage and commitment even in the midst of difficulty.

All of this can be part of the witness we make as we use this resource of singing in our life of prayer.

Reflecting and Recording

Why don't you try it now? If you are in a place where you can sing aloud, then sing the first hymn or Christian song that comes to your mind. If you are not in a place where you can sing out loud, sing it in your mind. Don't just remember the words in your mind; remember the tune to which the words are set. That is as close as you can get to singing out loud, and the music is as important as the words.

During the Day

Follow through on using this resource of song in praying. You will be in places during the day when you can sing. Then sing.

DAY SEVEN

Prayer and Action—"The Glory of God Is Each of Us Fully Alive!"

There is a certain class of demons that can only be chased away by prayer"—the demons of deafness to God, dumbness in thanksgiving, self-sufficiency, worry, despair, and solitude. But there is another class that can only be chased away by action—the demons of illusion, sentimentality, infantilism, narcissism, and laziness. So if we cultivate prayer exclusively, we harbor the second lot, and if we cultivate action exclusively, we harbor the first lot.

> Christianity leaves the famous and false distinction between action and contemplation far behind: it is participation; its prayer is love in action and its action is inspired by love. God is not the object and fixed goal of our quest; [God] is its active principle, cause, and motive power. Love is not made to be loved, but to be loving.[18]

On Day Six of last week we considered awareness as the primary meaning of praying without ceasing. The four dimensions of this awareness are awareness of self, awareness of others, awareness of the world, and awareness of God. The truth is that all these dimensions share an interrelatedness. No clear lines designate self-awareness or other-awareness or God-awareness. To be really alive is to be aware in all these dimensions. And "the glory of God," said Irenaeus, "is [each of us] fully alive."

Whatever techniques we use, the dynamic of prayer is communion with God. The goal of prayer is a life of friendship and fellowship with God, co-operation with God's Spirit, living God's life in the world. So we are considering in this final session the possibility of praying our lives.

Awareness is often painful because awareness always leads to sensitive involvement. That is the reason prayer can never be considered an isolated part of life. Jesus said, "Not everyone who says to me, 'Lord, Lord,' will enter the kingdom of heaven, but only the one who does the will of my Father" (Matt. 7:21)

Praying our lives means doing the will of the Father! Praying our lives means living God's life in the world! Praying our lives means modeling our lives after Jesus, the primary example of prayer-living! Praying our lives means *being* Christ to, or *receiving* Christ from, every person we meet!

Here it is from Jesus himself:

Matthew 25:34-40

Then the king will say to those at his right hand, "Come, you that are blessed by my Father, inherit the kingdom prepared for you from the foundation of the world; for I was hungry and you gave me food, I was thirsty and you gave me something to drink, I was a stranger and you welcomed me. . . ." Then the righteous will answer him, "Lord, when was it that we saw you hungry and gave you food, or thirsty and gave you something to drink? And when was it that we saw you a stranger and welcomed you, or naked and gave you clothing? And when was it that we saw you sick or in prison and visited you?" And the king will answer them, "Truly I tell you, just as you did it to one of the least of these who are members of my family, you did it to me."

The glory of God is each of us fully alive.

—Each of us alive to all the selves that are stirring within us, and to the struggle of Christ seeking to be "shaped within."
—Each of us alive to the Spirit, the image of God in others, God speaking to us through them, and to them through us!
—Each of us alive to the suffering of others and to the brokenness of life.
—Each of us alive to the possibility of reconciliation.
—Each of us alive to the events of history through which God is revealed to us.
—Each of us alive to all of creation "groaning" for perfection as the kingdom of God.

"The glory of God is each of us fully alive"—*alive to the living Christ.* Only in his power can we pray with our lives. Here is one who has loved the world and never left it. He came to bring himself, to bring us power to be and do what God wants us to be and do: "To all who received him, . . . he gave power to become children of God."

It is in Jesus' resurrected power that we are to pray with our lives. Jesus invites us to open ourselves to his energy and to go from this meager beginning to the triumph of experiencing the glory of God by being fully alive.

John 15:1-5

I am the true vine. . . . Abide in me as I abide in you. . . . You are the branches. Those who abide in me and I in them bear much fruit.

Reflecting and Recording

Think about what you have been experiencing for the past six weeks. List some of the most significant things that have happened to you.

What is your commitment now in relation to "praying with your life"?

Think about the persons who have shared this journey with you. Think of them one by one. Pray for them one by one. You may even want to perform some specific act of gratitude or appreciation for some of them who have been especially meaningful to you.

During the Day and the Coming Days

Put into practice all those things that "work" for you in making prayer a whole-life experience.

Group Meeting for Week Six

Introduction

Needs for group work: chalkboard, whiteboard, or newsprint

The "doing" dimension of prayer cannot be overemphasized. The old saying "To work is to pray" is true. It is also true that to pray is to work. Prayer is action. It is the integrating force of our being and doing.

The rhythm of action and reflection is the pattern of living prayer: being alone with God, reflecting upon how God comes to us, seeking God's will, appropriating God's strength, and acting according to what guidance and power we have—living God's life in the world by checking our signals with God and with fellow pilgrims.

If you are not continuing this as a group experience, you may wish to covenant with another person as "prayer partners," or you may have sensed that two or three in the group have a special interest in intercessory prayer. Before you leave the meeting, explore with them the possibility of a shared ministry of intercession.

If you are going to extend this adventure as a group, make your plans for meeting times and places and see that everyone has the resources the leader ordered.

Sharing Together

1. Share with the group your most meaningful day with the workbook this week.

2. Take a few minutes to reflect upon this six-week experience. Let each person make a brief, simple statement as to what difference this prayer adventure has made in his or her life. Select a person to record in a brief sentence or phrase each of these statements on a chalkboard, whiteboard, or on newsprint.

3. Let each person in the group share his or her greatest difficulty in making prayer part of a "living" experience.

4. What one "call" do you feel? Let each person voice what specific commitment to growth, change, or discipline he or she is willing to make.

5. Identify the one "action" to which your group (or two or three of you) may be corporately called. Write this on a chalkboard, whiteboard, or on newsprint.

Praying Together

Your praying together in this closing session should reflect as much of your total group experience as possible. Consider the following possibilities.

For the needs of persons:

1. Each person takes a turn in a chair in the center of the room. Let all the group lay hands on that person, with those who wish offering verbal prayers that reflect your experience with that person during this six weeks. Give each person, as he or she comes to the chair, the opportunity to voice a need that may not have yet surfaced in the group, but which he or she is now willing to share.

2. Sometimes persons with problems—anxiety, fear, or distrust—can be ministered to by entrusting themselves to the group to confirm trust. A person may lie on the floor and allow the group literally to raise him or her up and be lifted into the air in commitment to God. It is amazing what such an experience of trust can do for a person, and how such a vivid memory of being lifted to God in prayer can take a person into the future with strength.

For the affirmation of persons:

At the heart of prayer is our faith in a loving Father who wants to give us good gifts. You may wish to have each person in the group receive "good gifts" from fellow pilgrims as an affirmation of God's love and care. Let each person, in turn, be the recipient of "good gifts." (Example: Mary is our recipient. What gifts will we give her? Think about who Mary is, what she has contributed to the group, what needs and concerns she has expressed. Let as many as wish to do so verbalize and perhaps act out the giving of these gifts. Someone may wish to hold Mary's hands and say, "Mary, receive God's gift of forgiveness. Be free of the burden of guilt about your feeling of failure as a mother." Then someone else may wish to give Mary a gift by saying to Mary across the room, "Mary, I affirm you as a caring person and want to give you patience. Be patient with yourself, for God is patient with you.") Before you close your meeting consider what has been recorded about each person's experience in this six weeks, as well as the group commitment. Find some way to celebrate these breakthroughs.

Closing the meeting

Last week we passed the peace as our benediction, our blessing in parting. This week close your meeting with a more spontaneous blessing. Go to every person in the group; say and do whatever you feel is appropriate for your parting blessing to this person. You may shake hands and say, "May you always be sensitive to the blessing of God's presence with you." Or you may hold both hands of the person, look him or her in the eyes and say, "I love you and I know God loves you." Or you may simply embrace the person and say nothing. In your own unique way, "bless" each person who has shared this journey with you.

APPENDIX

Three Additional Weeks of Study

The suggestions for these three additional weeks center around *resources* for living prayer. Each week is an experiment with a particular resource.

Out of your six weeks together you will have discovered meaningful ways of relating and sharing. Even though some specific suggestions for your group meetings are included here, they are deliberately limited. You have the leadership and the creative ability in your group to continue not only these three weeks but as long as your life together in this venture is meaningful.

For Week Nine your group may purchase one or more of The Upper Room Spiritual Classics. These small volumes introduce some of the "great models" to be used. You may order by calling Upper Room Books at 1-800-972-0433 or by ordering online at bookstore.upperroom.org.

Week Seven: Praying with the Scripture

As we begin Week Seven the format will differ. Insert additional blank pages in your workbook. Read at one sitting this section for Week Seven.

For the first four days of this week you will use the method of discovery with which you experimented on Day Three of Week Five (page 127) and Day Two of Week Six (page 153). Review those experiments now. The scripture suggestions for the first four days of this week are: Day One: Isaiah 6:1-6; Day Two: Luke 4:1-13; Day Three: Luke 4:14-21; and Day Four: 1 Peter 2:1-10.

Reflect and record daily by using the three personal discovery questions for these first four days. For the remaining three days of this week, pray with the scripture by "being quiet before the Word." Go back and review Day Three of Week Six (page 157). Use the following scriptures: Day Five: Luke 12:13-21; Day Six: Matthew 18:21-35; and Day Seven: Matthew 25:31-46.

Group Sharing

Begin your time together by asking each person to share the most meaningful message he or she received from the scripture and in prayer this week. Then let each person in the group select one of the first four passages and share his or her response to the question, "If I decided to act upon the message of this scripture, what would it mean?"

Let persons who are willing share their response to "being quiet before the Word" that they wrote on either Day Five, Six, or Seven.

In your praying together, focus on the needs that are reflected in what people feel called to be and to do in response to a particular scripture.

Week Eight: Praying the Psalms

Review Day Four of Week Six (page 160).

Begin at the first psalm and read until a particular psalm or portion of a psalm grabs your attention. Reflect upon it, relating it to where you are at this time in your life.

Copy that portion of scripture on blank pages you have inserted in your workbook. Then as you reflect on it, write your personal response. You may be called to confession or praise. You may be inspired to write some poetry or even a hymn. You may be pushed to make a commitment to action. Record your response.

On the following day begin reading the Psalms where you left off and continue until the Word gets your attention; pray in response to that passage. Continue this pattern each day this week.

Group Sharing

When you come together as a group, make sure that everyone has an opportunity to share. One way to do this is for each individual to select the experiences of one day, as recorded in the workbook, that he or she is willing to share with the group. Let every person share, with the group responding to the person.

Let your praying together be spontaneous and grow out of your sharing. Before closing, let persons select from the Spiritual Classics the book they will live for the following week. (A list of the titles available is found in the Bibliography on page 182.)

Week Nine: "Soaking Our Souls in the Great Models"

Spend your prayer time the first day of this week reading the classic you selected. Read the biographical sketch and excerpt(s) in one sitting. Spiritual Classics editor Keith Beasley-Topliffe advises you to (1) Read to learn. Approach the text as a student. Don't be distracted by the author's peculiarities or theological differences. Just try to hear his or her core message. (2) Read slowly. Reread passages that appeal to you. *Reflect and record* what the passage says to you. (3) Read bravely. Pay attention to passages that disturb you and ponder why.

Above all, try to catch the spirit of the writer—"soak your soul" in this model. Be prepared to share with your group the ideas or insights you have received. Select a brief passage or a prayer from the book that is meaningful to you.

Group Sharing

Let each person share what he or she has received from the chosen classic. Participants may wish to read aloud the brief passage they selected. After each reading, allow quiet time for personal reflection. Ask someone to close the session with prayer.

THE GLORY OF GOD IS EACH OF US FULLY ALIVE!

Ask, and it will be given you; search, and you will find; knock, and the door will be opened for you. For everyone who asks receives, and everyone who searches finds, and for everyone who knocks, the door will be opened.

(Matthew 7:7-8)

Day by day, O dear Lord,
Three things I pray:
to see thee more clearly,
love thee more dearly,
follow thee more nearly,
day by day, by day, by day.

Whoever would approach [God] must believe that he exists and that he rewards those who seek him.

(Hebrews 11:6)

Those who wait for the LORD shall renew their strength, they shall mount up with wings like eagles,
they shall run and not be weary,
they shall walk and not faint.

(Isaiah 40:31)

The secret is simply this:
Christ in _____
(your name)

Yes, Christ in [me] bringing with him the hope of all the glorious things to come.

(Colossians 1:27, PHILLIPS)

NOTES

1. Harry Emerson Fosdick, *The Meaning of Prayer* (New York: Association Press, 1963, 37–38.

2. Ibid., 34.

3. John B. Cobb, Jr., *To Pray or Not to Pray* (Nashville, TN: The Upper Room, 1974), 25.

4. Fosdick, *The Meaning of Prayer*, 55.

5. Lewis Maclachlan, *The Teaching of Jesus on Prayer* (London: James Clarke and Company, Ltd., 1952), 14.

6. Gerhard Ebeling, *On Prayer* (Philadelphia: Fortress Press, 1966), 50.

7. Douglas Steere, *Dimensions of Prayer* (New York: Woman's Division of Christian Service, Board of Missions, The Methodist Church, 1962), 58.

8. Maclachlan, *The Teaching of Jesus on Prayer*, 25.

9. Fosdick, *The Meaning of Prayer*, 182.

10. Steere, *Dimensions of Prayer*, 83.

11. Fosdick, *The Meaning of Prayer*, 183.

12. Frank C. Laubach, *Pray for Others* (Nashville, TN: The Upper Room, 1947), 19.

13. Maxie D. Dunnam, *Be Your Whole Self* (Atlanta: Forum House Publishers, 1970), 97.

14. Tom and Edna Boone, *Prayer and Action* (Nashville, TN: The Upper Room, 1974), 9–10.

15. Steere, *Dimensions of Prayer*, 25–26.

16. Frank Laubach, *Letters by a Modern Mystic* (Westwood, N.J.: Fleming H. Revell Co., 1958), 27–28.

17. J. Minton Batten, *Selections from the Writings of St. Francis of Assisi* (Nashville: The Upper Room, 1952), 36.

18. Louis Evely, *Our Prayer* (New York: Herder and Herder, Inc., 1970), 106–107.

BIBLIOGRAPHY

Classics

à Kempis, Thomas. *On the Imitation of Christ.* London: Oxford University Press, 1909.

Brother Lawrence. *The Practice of the Presence of God.* Nashville: The Upper Room, 1950.

Buttrick, George A. *Prayer.* New York: Abingdon Press, 1942.

Fosdick, Harry E. *The Meaning of Prayer.* London: Student Christian Movement Press, 1918.

Herman, E. *Creative Prayer.* London: James Clarke and Co., Ltd., 1926.

Kelly, Thomas R. *A Testament of Devotion.* New York: Harper and Brothers, 1941.